Aboriginal Population Profiles for Development Planning in the Northern East Kimberley

J. Taylor

THE AUSTRALIAN NATIONAL UNIVERSITY

E PRESS

Centre for Aboriginal Economic Policy Research
The Australian National University, Canberra

Research Monograph No. 23
2003

ANU

E PRESS

Published by ANU E P ress
The Australian National University
Canberra ACT 0200, Australia
Email: anuepress@anu.edu.au
Web: http://epress.anu.edu.au

Previously published by the
Centre for Aboriginal Economic Policy Research,
The Australian National University

National Library of Australia
Cataloguing-in-publication entry.

Aboriginal Population Profiles for Development Planning in the Northern East Kimberley

ISBN 1 9209420 8 4
ISBN 1 9209420 3 3 (Online document)

1. Aboriginal Australians - Western Australia - Kimberley - Population. 2. Aboriginal Australians - Western Australia - Kimberley - Economic conditions. 3. Aboriginal Australians - Western Australia - Kimberley - Social conditions. 4. Kimberley (W.A.) - Economic conditions. 5. Kimberley (W.A.) - Social conditions. I. Title.

305.8991509414

Designed by Green Words & Images (GWi)
Cover design by Brendon McKinley

First edition © 2003 Centre for Aboriginal Economic Policy Research
This edition © 2004 ANU E Press

Foreword

This monograph had its genesis in approaches made by Argyle Diamond Mine (ADM) in 2001 to John Taylor to develop a social and economic profile of the population resident within an area potentially influenced by the mine's presence. This research task was similar to one he prepared for Rio Tinto Ltd in the previous year in south-east Arnhem Land subsequently enhanced and published as CAEPR Monograph No. 18 *Ngukurr at the Millennium: A Baseline Profile for Social Impact Planning in South-East Arnhem Land* (J. Taylor, J. Bern and K.A. Senior). However, practical steps in pursuit of ADM's research objective were not taken until the Kimberley Land Council commissioned the present study late in 2002. This research was an important part of their compilation of strategic information to assist in negotiations with ADM for the development of a new comprehensive Indigenous Land Use Agreement. Both of these requests emerged following revised assessments of possible underground mining at Argyle.

The outcome is a statistical analysis of social and economic conditions among Indigenous and non-Indigenous residents of the northern part of the East Kimberley. The data presented describe the situation in 2001, 20 years after the commencement of mining at Argyle and at a point in time when choices are to be made either to extend mining activities or to wind them down ahead of eventual closure. Either way, Taylor's comprehensive profile provides invaluable input to discussions about mining impacts on regional economies by quantifying the changes that have occurred since mining commenced, and in projecting some likely future social and economic outcomes. To this extent, it is also instructive for the East Kimberley Indigenous Communities Coordination Pilot (ICCP) trial project sponsored by the Council of Australian Governments and overseen by the Commonwealth Department of Transport and Regional Services, as it demonstrates the range of data that can be compiled on a regional scale in that part of Western Australia.

This monograph also has important links to another project, 'Community Organisations and Miners: Partnering Sustainable Regional Development?' an ARC Linkage project between CAEPR, Rio Tinto Ltd and the Committee for Economic Development of Australia (CEDA). This project, that began in 2002 and will run until 2006, is seeking to assess the potential development impacts of mines at a number of locations in remote Australia.

By publishing this report in the CAEPR Research Monograph series we aim to ensure timely and wide distribution of these research findings throughout the Indigenous policy community. All too often, vital benchmark statistical information gathered in the course of impact assessment work remains either unpublished or relatively inaccessible. The same will not be said of the present analysis. We would like to acknowledge the role of ADM in financially supporting this research and its publication in the present format.

Professor Jon Altman
Director, CAEPR
December 2003

Acknowledgments

Such a wide-ranging, data-driven study is necessarily a collaborative venture drawing upon the goodwill and resources of numerous individuals and agencies. Those who contributed most to this endeavour include Cath Elderton, Allan Wedderburn, and Archie Tanna of the Kimberley Land Council in Kununurra, along with Andy Munro of Rio Tinto Ltd in Perth, all of whom facilitated the smooth running of various stages of the project. Cath Elderton, in particular, was vitally important in identifying the need for baseline data and coordinating the fieldwork stage in the East Kimberley. Agency assistance consisted largely of the provision and interpretation of data. In this regard, thanks are due to numerous individuals across Western Australia—in Kununurra, Jon Bok and Mike Britz of ATSIC, Jamie Treloar of Centrelink, Jeff Gooding of the Kimberley Development Commission, Alan Hubbard from KREAC CDEP, and Kim Morrish at the Ord Valley Aboriginal Health Service; at Argyle Diamond Mine, Daniel Archer from the Community Relations Unit and David Epworth from the Regional Business Development Unit; in Wyndham, Reg Birch at Joorak Ngarni CDEP, Jim Lewis of the Wyndham Action Group, and Dianna Spyker and Gerald Mills at the Business Enterprise Centre; in Woolah, Rebecca Sampi at Woolah Community School; in Warmun, Max Thomas from Warmun Community Council, Sister Alma at Ngalangangpum School, Rick Chapman at Warmun CDEP, and the management at Warmun Arts Centre; in Halls Creek, Michael Quall at Ngoongjuwah CDEP, Peter McConnel from Halls Creek Shire Council, and Ian Benjamin at Yuri Yangi Medical Service; in Broome, Sue Metcalfe from the Kimberley Aboriginal Medical Services Council; in Perth, Frank Parriman and Kati Krizla, from the Department of Justice; John Loh and Anna Ferrante from the Crime Research Unit at the University of Western Australia who provided invaluable assistance in the interpretation of regional crime statistics; Ron Dullard of the Catholic Education Office; Angela Harris, Susie Brown, and Stephen Humphrey from the Western Australian Department of Education and Training; Luke Drozdowski, from the Office of Training; Sue Eslick, Jim Codde, Sylvie Price and Pam Olney from the Department of Health; Trevor Tann and Tom Mulholland from the Department of Indigenous Affairs; Robin Wood from the Department of Housing and Works; and Gary Paterson from the Department of Mineral and Petroleum Resources who greatly assisted by coordinating this whole of government response. Also, at the ABS in Perth, Deborah Wade-Marshall and Chris Spencer helped with the provision of population estimates and census data. A final note of thanks is due to Bruce Harvey of Rio Tinto Ltd and Simon Nish of Argyle Diamonds for their foresight in supporting the research venture and in subsidising the cost of converting a research report into this monograph.

Contents

List of figures and tables

Figures

Tables

Abbreviations and acronyms

ABS	Australian Bureau of Statistics
ADM	Argyle Diamond Mine
ASGC	Australian Standard Geographic Classification
ASR	age-standardised rate
ATSIC	Aboriginal and Torres Strait Islander Commission
CD	Collection District
CDEP	Community Development Employment Projects (scheme)
CHINS	Community Housing and Infrastructure Needs Survey
CHIP	Community Housing and Infrastructure Program
CHIPS	Children's Court and Petty Sessions
CRC	Crime Research Centre
DEWR	Department of Employment and Workplace Relations
DHW	Department of Housing and Works
EHNS	Environmental Health Needs Survey
EKIAP	East Kimberley Impact Assessment Project
ERMP	(Ashton Joint Venture) Environmental Review and Management Program
ERP	Estimated Resident Population
FI/FO	fly-in/fly-out (workers)
GNP	Good Neighbour Program
HIPP	Health Infrastructure Priority Projects
IA	Indigenous Area
ICD	International Classification of Diseases
ILUA	Indigenous Land Use Agreement
KAMSC	Kimberley Aboriginal Medical Services Council
KHS	Kimberley Health Services
KLC	Kimberley Land Council
KRSIS	Kakadu Region Social Impact Study

LGA	Local Government Area
MLCR	module load completion rate
NAHS	National Aboriginal Health Strategy
NATSIS	National Aboriginal and Torres Strait Islander Survey
NCEPH	National Centre for Epidemiology and Population Health
NHMRC	National Health and Medical Research Council
NHS	National Health Survey
NILF	not in the labour force
OECD	Organisation for Economic Cooperation and Development
OVAHS	Ord Valley Aboriginal Health Service
QOL	quality of life
SIA	Social Impact Assessment
SLA	Statistical Local Area
STD	sexually transmitted disease
TAFE	Technical and Futher Education
TFR	Total Fertility Rate
TOMS	Total Offender Management System
VET	Vocational Education and Training
WALNA	Western Australian Literacy and Numeracy Assessment (program)
WHO	World Health Organisation

1. Analytical framework

This study develops and presents social indicators for the population resident within a region (referred to here as the Northern East Kimberley region) defined as relevant to the purposes of constructing a new comprehensive agreement over future activities in the Argyle Diamond Mine (ADM) lease area in the East Kimberley. Its initial aim was to provide statistical input to assist negotiations towards this agreement as well as to provide a baseline against which subsequent monitoring of the impact of any agreement could take place. It is presented here, however, with a much broader remit as a case study in regional statistical profiling for general public policy deliberation about future development directions in one of Western Australia's poorest regions.

The current process of agreement-making between ADM and the Kimberley Land Council (KLC) marks something of a crossroads for communities in the region as it comes almost 25 years after the commencement of mining-related activities at Barramundi Gap, at a time when decisions are to be made about either extending these activities with underground production into the next decade, or commencing a period of wind-down in pit and processing operations leading to mine closure by around 2010. Either way, further social and economic impacts on communities close to the mine site, as well as those in the wider region, are to be expected, given the prominent role that ADM has played to date in the East Kimberley economy.

Developments in the agricultural, tourism and service sectors have also contributed substantially to socio-economic change in the East Kimberley in recent times, and will continue to do so in the future. However, the decision to extend or cease mining operations at ADM warrants special public policy attention in light of the often fraught history of relations between the mine and local Aboriginal communities, and the existence (since 2001) of a Memorandum of Understanding between ADM and the KLC which sets out the steps towards a new comprehensive Indigenous Land Use Agreement (ILUA). Such an agreement will attempt to ensure that the consequences of on-going ADM activities are managed and not arbitrary, and that appropriate benefits flow to traditional owners, local communities and the wider region.

In this process, the establishment of baseline data on social and economic conditions was seen by the KLC and ADM as an essential component of Social Impact Assessment (SIA). As one contributor to previous impact assessment in the East Kimberley has put it, such assessment constitutes an area of systematic inquiry which seeks to investigate and understand the social and economic consequences of planned change and the processes involved in that change (Ross 1990). Analysis of this type has an established history in the region (Coombs et al. 1989; Dillon 1990; Dixon et al. 1990) having emerged as an essential feature of the public policy response to the initial development of ADM. Whilst this response occurred largely at the insistence of local Aboriginal communities (Dillon 1990), the need for monitoring of social and economic conditions is now enshrined in Rio Tinto policy governing relations with local communities (Harvey 2002). It is also a requirement of the Environmental Protection Statement for the ADM Underground Project. Accordingly, the current political economy of mining in the region demands that Indigenous communities more fully avail themselves of any economic opportunities that arise (Harvey 2002).

In this regard, the key initiative to date in the Northern East Kimberley region has been the original Glen Hill (Argyle) Agreement subsequently extended by the Good Neighbour Program (GNP) the goal of which was to improve the circumstances of the communities (at Mandangala, Woolah, and Warmun) closest to the Argyle mine site. While the present deliberations towards a more comprehensive ILUA continue to include these same groups, there is increasing recognition by stakeholders that realisation of the benefits of mining to local populations, both in the production phase and beyond, requires the development of a sustainable mixed regional economy. This, in turn, necessitates the inclusion of an enhanced Indigenous capacity to engage and participate in the regional economy. Such intent necessarily widens the scope of any impact analysis beyond the relatively narrow geographic focus of the GNP to encompass a more functional definition of 'area affected' based on some measure of regionally integrated social, economic and administrative interactions.

The need for such a wider geographic perspective in assessing the impacts and potential benefits of mining formed part of a critique of the Glen Hill Agreement from the outset. According to Dixon (1990: 68), this critique was constructed by those disaffected by the signing of the Good Neighbour Agreement in terms of a perceived failure on the part of the Ashton Joint Venture company to discharge its obligations fully to people entitled to share in the material benefits of the mine's development. This failure was perceived in terms of *wunan*, a word used in the region to refer to the network of trading relationships across the region that exists for the purposes of ritualised barter (Palmer and Williams 1990: 10). This network extends a set of reciprocal rights and obligations between Aboriginal people throughout the East Kimberley from the stations around the Halls Creek area, north through the Ord Valley catchment to Kununurra, Wyndham, and further to Kalumburu (not to mention areas beyond, to the west Kimberley and into the Northern Territory) (Dixon 1990: 84). Significantly, in reflecting on the Glen Hill Agreement, Dixon (1990: 83) cites an Aboriginal view expressed at the time that royalties and other benefits from mining activity were viewed as *wunan*. While this concept is not used here to circumscribe a region of interest, it nonetheless reinforces the idea of profiling social and economic circumstances over a region that is considerably wider than just the areas adjacent to the mine site.

Further rationale for this regional approach derives from the intent of modern mining agreements, as these aim to assist in the establishment of diversified economic activity in the vicinity of mine sites that is sustainable beyond the life of mining activity (Harvey 2002). One question that arises in this context is the degree to which mines, such as Argyle, already contribute to regional development, and to what extent they might do so in the future, particularly by generating a source of local employment both on and off the mine site. In answering this, some idea of what mines do not and cannot contribute to regional development is also provided.

Methods

The standard approach to SIA involves post-facto assessment of social and economic change consequent upon development interventions. While this is also attempted here, the focus is much more on profiling current conditions in the region, not just to compare with the past, but also to establish a baseline against which future social and economic change might be calibrated. To this end, a predictive capacity is sought through the use of projections of future population and jobs growth, thereby laying a foundation for social impact planning as much as social impact assessment. While these tasks seem straightforward enough, the manner in which they have been carried out in particular cases has varied considerably (Coombs et al. 1989; Kesteven 1986; Kakadu Region Social Impact Study (KRSIS) 1997; Taylor, Bern and Senior 1999). In the present study, the aim is to statistically profi le the socio-economic status of the Aboriginal and non-Aboriginal populations of the region at the commencement of mining at Argyle (1981, as dictated by data availability), to draw comparison with an equivalent profile for the present (as at 2001, again for reasons of data availability). The aim is to develop regional population projections from the present to 2016 so as to anticipate the extent and nature of social policy needs in the Northern East Kimberley over much of the possible span of mining activity at Argyle and any agreements associated with it.

In constructing these statistical profiles, a range of social indicators were compiled using data from a variety of published and unpublished sources which included the Census of Population and Housing, administrative data sets held by the Aboriginal and Torres Strait Islander Commission (ATSIC), Commonwealth and Western Australian government departments, locally-based Aboriginal organisations, ADM, and other regionally-based institutions such as schools, Shire councils, and businesses. This process was greatly assisted by the KLC, as well as by consultations with key informants both within regional communities and in relevant agencies in Perth, Kununurra, Wyndham, Halls Creek, Warmun, Broome and Canberra. Because of the specific focus on generating statistical information, reference to literature that describes aspects of social and economic life in the region, both past and present, is limited to instances where this provides a key source of statistical data or assists in its interpretation.

The scope of the profile covers key social and economic features of the Aboriginal and non-Aboriginal components of the regional population that typically form the basis of policy interest and potential intervention. These include demographic structure and residence patterns, labour force status, education and training, income, welfare, housing, justice and health status. For each of these categories, the aim is to identify and describe the main characteristics of the population and to highlight outstanding features in the data. While assessment of change in each of these is one aim, this is only possible where reliable time series can be compiled. Surprisingly, given the extent of previous impact assessment in this region, relatively little statistical information is available in the public domain with which to portray social and economic conditions at the outset of mining.

All sources of social indicator data have drawbacks in terms of providing a meaningful representation of the social and economic status of Aboriginal people in the region. With census data, for example, there are concerns about the cultural relevance of information obtained from an instrument principally designed to establish the characteristics of mainstream Australian life (Smith 1991). Thus, having observed the 2001 Census count first hand at a Northern Territory outstation, Frances Morphy (2002) has described the process of enumeration as a 'collision of systems' concluding that census questions lack cross-cultural fit and produce answers that are often close to nonsensical.

Economic status, for example, would seem to be an unproblematic concept. In mainstream society this is generally measured by indicators such as cash income and levels of ownership of assets. However, among many Aboriginal groups it is often measured in quite different ways. For example, as pointed out by Altman (2000: 3-4), in some tradition-oriented communities a person's status can be largely determined by access to ritual or religious knowledge rather than to material resources. Similarly, social status can be accrued by controlling the distribution of material resources rather than being an accumulator (or owner) of resources (Altman 2000: 3). In short, materialistic considerations may be of less importance among sections of the Aboriginal population, where the emphasis is rather on reciprocity in economic relations (Schwab 1995).

Equally, while social indicators report on observable population characteristics, they reveal nothing about more behavioural population attributes such as individual and community priorities and aspirations for enhancing quality of life. Indeed the whole question of what this might mean anyway and how it can be measured in an Aboriginal domain has yet to be addressed, although exploratory work on local measurement of such concepts as community strength (Memmott and Meltzer 2003) and health status (Senior 2003) provide some initial guidance here. Nor do formal indicators adequately capture the complexity of social arrangements between individuals, families and households. For example, census data identify discrete dwellings as households, but the basic economic and social units of consumption in remote Aboriginal communities are often comprised of linked households rather than single ones (Smith 2000).

Defining the region

A key issue for social impact assessment is the question of how to define areas or populations affected by particular past, present, and future development projects. While complete resolution of the issue may not be possible, contemplation of it is more than just academic—it has practical consequences for the construction of spatial boundaries that may either facilitate or impede access to relevant data for impact assessment.

For the present analysis, it just so happens that a geographic area of interest was specified by the KLC. Fortunately, this area (the Northern East Kimberley) corresponds to select statistical boundaries (or at least to a composite thereof) that are contained within the Australian Standard Geographic Classification (ASGC) of the Australian Bureau of Statistics (ABS). Accordingly, this provides a basis for compiling population characteristics and constructing social indicators.

As shown in Figure 1.1, the study region incorporates that part of the East Kimberley which commences at Halls Creek and extends northwards through Oombulgurri to Kalumburu, with the Northern Territory border as the eastern boundary. As such, it covers much of the traditional lands of the Gija and Miriuwung-Gajerong peoples.

It also effectively encompasses the East Kimberley's three major towns and centres of economic activity (Kununurra, Wyndham and Halls Creek), and all of its major discrete Aboriginal communities and associated outstations (except for those in the more arid region to the south of Halls Creek). In effect, it comprises that part of the Kimberley for which Kununurra is the primary service centre. Thus, as Figure 1.1 illustrates, the region of interest forms only part of the wider Wunan ATSIC region, and incorporates the whole of the Wyndham-East Kimberley Statistical Local Area (SLA), but only half of the Halls Creek SLA. This incorporates nine Indigenous Areas (IAs)—Kalumburu, Oombulgurri, Wyndham, Wyndham-East Kimberley (S) west, Kununurra, Lake Argyle, Warmun, Halls Creek (S) north, and Halls Creek), and 10 Indigenous Locations (all of the IAs, plus Woolah).

Figure 1.1. Statistical geography of the East Kimberley and Northern East Kimberley

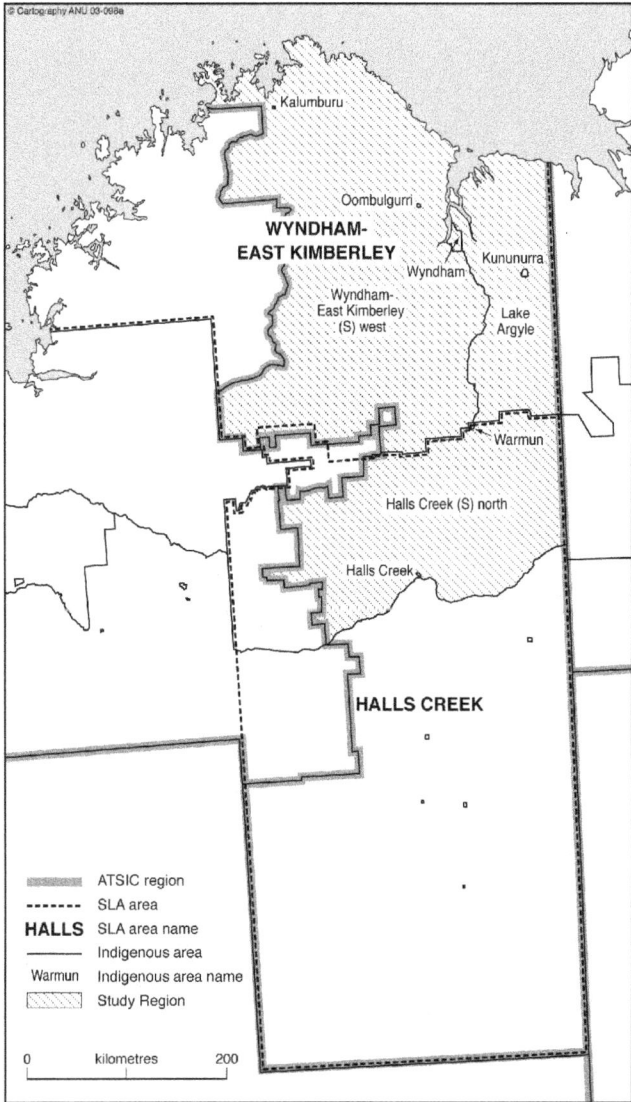

It should be noted that this varies somewhat from the geographic focus of the earlier East Kimberley Impact Assessment Project (EKIAP) which extended further southwards to Malan and excluded areas north of Wyndham (Coombs et al. 1989: xvi). In adopting this geography, this is not to deny that the social reality, especially for Aboriginal people, is one of social, cultural, and economic interconnectedness between this region and adjacent lands. One manifestation of this is the frequent movement of individuals, groups and families into and out of the region, making clear definition of a 'regional' population problematic.

2. Demography of the East Kimberley and Northern East Kimberley

A range of counts and estimates are available for the Indigenous and non-Indigenous populations of the East Kimberley. For example, the ABS provides a *de facto* count of people who were deemed to be present in the region on census night (7 August 2001 at the most recent census). Then, there is a *de jure* count of people across Australia who indicated that one of the two East Kimberley SLAs was their usual place of residence on census night. These two counts are also available for Indigenous Areas found within the Northern East Kimberley. Finally, in recognition of the fact that the census fails to count some people, the ABS develops post-censual estimates of the 'true' population by augmenting their SLA 'usual residence' counts according to an estimate of those missed (net undercount), as well as other demographic adjustments. This produces an Estimated Resident Population (ERP), which in effect becomes the official population of each SLA for the purposes of electoral representation and financial distributions.

It should be emphasised that official ERPs are only available at the SLA-level. Estimates of the population within the study region, and its constituent parts, therefore have to be derived by ratio allocation of the overall ERP for the two East Kimberley SLAs combined. In terms of the present exercise, and in regard to the quite separate structural circumstances of most Indigenous people in the region, it is helpful that separate calculations of Indigenous and non-Indigenous ERPs have also been made by the ABS (since 1996) using differential undercount rates, and by distributing (pro rata) those usual residents who did not answer the ethnicity question on the census form.

One difficulty with the measurement of demographic change in the region since operations at Argyle commenced more than 20 years ago is the fact that the ABS has altered its statistical geography in this area several times during this period. Although the two Local Government Areas (LGAs, more recently described as Statistical Local Areas—SLAs) of Wyndham-East Kimberley and Halls Creek have remained intact, many collection district (CD) boundaries have changed substantially and the number of CDs has also varied with far more in existence now than 20 years ago. Additional geography was introduced in 1996 with the creation of IAs, and their sub-category Indigenous Locations (ABS 1998a), for the purposes of disseminating Indigenous community profile data (including data for the non-Indigenous population). As shown in Figure 1.1, this provides for reasonably fine-grained analysis down to the level of most communities of interest, with the main exception of Mandangala which forms part of the Lake Argyle IA.

Thus, in some cases, Indigenous (and non-Indigenous) profile data are available for specific communities and towns (viz Kalumburu, Oombulgurri, Wyndham, Kununurra, Woolah, Warmun and Halls Creek), whereas other smaller communities (such as Mandangala and all outstation communities) are subsumed as part of larger geographic units (Wyndham-East Kimberley (S) west, Lake Argyle, and Halls Creek (S) North) (ABS 2002a). However, since 1992, the ABS has endeavoured to gather information on estimated population numbers for all discrete Indigenous communities[1], no matter how small, via the Community Housing and Infrastructure Needs Survey (CHINS). A prototype CHINS was developed on a state-by-state basis in 1992, followed by more nationally integrated surveys in 1999 and 2001.

It should also be noted that alongside these ABS geographic units, various regional service providers construct population lists of clients drawn from often quite different catchment areas. In Halls Creek, for example, the Yuri Yangi Medical Service caters for the town of Halls Creek as well as many outlying settlements, most of which lie to the south and beyond the region of interest. In Kununurra, the Ord Valley Aboriginal Medical Service is utilised by individuals from as far as Kalumburu, as well as across the Northern Territory border. Schools tend to have highly localised catchments for primary level students, but data for the high schools at Wyndham, Kununurra and Halls Creek are necessarily a composite of students from much wider areas. Participants in individual Community Development Employment Project (CDEP) schemes may also be spread among a number of communities.

Population size

At the 2001 Census, a total of 13,854 persons were counted by the ABS as present on census night (7 August) in the two East-Kimberley SLAs of Wyndham-East Kimberley and Halls Creek (Table 2.1). Of these, 5,249 indicated an Indigenous status in response to the census question on ethnicity, and 7,115 indicated non-Indigenous status. With as many as 1,490 individuals (11%) providing no response to this question, their Indigenous status remains indeterminate. Of the entire population counted within Australia on census night, a smaller total (10,757) nominated one of these East Kimberley SLAs as their usual place of residence.

Table 2.1. Indigenous and non-Indigenous census counts and post-censual estimates: East Kimberley region,[a] 2001

	Indigenous	Non-Indigenous	Not Stated	Total
Census count (de facto)	5,249	7,115	1,490	13,854
Usual residence count (de jure)	5,226	4,224	1,307	10,757
Estimated usual residents (ERP)[b]	6,000	5,176	Pro rated	11,176

Notes: a. Wyndham-East Kimberley, and Halls Creek SLAs combined

b. Preliminary estimates only

Source: ABS customised tables

Also indicated in Table 2.1 is the fact that the number of Indigenous usual residents of the East Kimberley was slightly lower than those counted as present there on census night. However, the number of non-Indigenous usual residents counted was substantially lower (by 41%) than the place of enumeration count. On this evidence, almost half of the non-Indigenous population present in the East Kimberley at any given time is visiting the region from elsewhere in Australia, at least during the dry season when the census is conducted. Given this scale of visitation, plus the fact that these visitors to the region may have somewhat different characteristics from those resident in the region, any comparative analysis of regional population characteristics that informs social impact assessment should be conducted using usual residence data only.

At the time of writing only preliminary ERP figures for the East Kimberley were available and these are shown in the final row of Table 2.1. As noted earlier, these purport to represent 'true' levels of the Indigenous and non-Indigenous populations of the region. However, when interpreting these, it is important to note that ABS ERPs have been observed to differ from other (unofficial) population estimates generated by alternate means (Taylor and Bell 2001, 2003). It is also necessary to take into account those methodological tendencies within the special procedures adopted by the ABS in remote communities and urban town camps in Northern Australia that are likely to produce an undercount of Indigenous people (Martin and Taylor 1996; Sanders 2002). It is debatable whether the standard ERP methodology adequately compensates for these shortcomings (Taylor and Bell 2003).

The study region

As noted, ERP figures are only available at SLA-level. One way to develop similar estimates of the population resident in the study region, and in each of its constituent parts, is to divide up the East Kimberley Indigenous and non-Indigenous ERPs, as reported above, according to the observed pro rata share of the relevant Indigenous Areas. Results of this ratio allocation are shown in Table 2.2. Thus, the Indigenous usual residence count in Kununurra (755) represented 16.8% of the Indigenous usual residence count for the whole of the East Kimberley. This same percentage of the East Kimberley Indigenous ERP produces an Indigenous population estimate for Kununurra of 1,009. In turn, the equivalent non-Indigenous proportion is 56.5%, which produces an estimate of 2,923 for the non-Indigenous population of Kununurra. All told, then, the 2001 total ERP of Kununurra is calibrated at almost 3,932, one quarter of whom are Indigenous.

Applying this methodology throughout, the resident population of the Northern East Kimberley is estimated at 9,259 in 2001, almost half of which (4,317) is Indigenous. These derived estimates for the Indigenous and non-Indigenous populations are not inconsequential as they are 22% and 27% higher than the reported census usual residence counts respectively.

Table 2.2.   Ratio allocation of the 2001 East Kimberley ERP to Indigenous Areas in the Northern East Kimberley

Indigenous Area	Indigenous % of E-Kim UR count	Non-Indigenous % of E-Kim UR resident	Derived Indigenous ERP	Derived Non-Indigenous ERP	Derived total ERP	Indigenous % of total derived ERP
Kununurra	16.8	56.5	1,009	2,923	3,932	25.7
Wyndham	10.3	7.2	617	374	991	62.3
Oombulgurri	3.2	0.3	193	15	208	92.8
Kalumburu	5.3	0.9	319	46	365	87.5
Lake Argyle	4.5	20.2	270	1,046	1,316	20.5
W/E-Kim (W)	2.8	2.0	169	102	271	62.2
Woolah	0.9	0.1	54	3	57	94.4
Warmun	5.4	0.6	324	31	355	91.2
Halls Creek	18.9	5.7	1,131	294	1,425	79.4
Halls Creek (N)	3.8	2.1	231	108	339	68.2
Study region	71.9	95.5	4,317	4,942	9,259	46.5

Note: UR = usual residence

A striking feature of these estimates is the fact that most areas of the Northern East Kimberley have overwhelmingly Aboriginal populations. The main exceptions are the Kununurra and Lake Argyle Indigenous Areas where the demographic influence of urban development and the Argyle mine are in evidence. The overall effect of this is to reduce the Aboriginal share of population in the Northern East Kimberley to less than 50%—clearly a misleading statistic that does not account for the demographic influence of Kununurra and the Argyle mine site. Also worth noting is the fact that 72% of the Indigenous population resident in the East Kimberley as a whole is located within this Northern region. This compares to 95% of the non-Indigenous population.

Population growth

East Kimberley

Time series analysis of these estimated populations is rendered problematic by changes in census geography at the small area level. However, it is possible to adjust Indigenous and non-indigenous ERPs for the whole of the East Kimberley for the period 1981 to 1991 to account for those who did not report their Indigenous status, and then to apply an approximation of census undercount based on the levels suggested by the 1996 and 2001 ERPs. The results of this manipulation are shown in Table 2.3. The same data are shown graphically in Figure 2.1.

Table 2.3. Derived[a] and actual ERPs[b] by Indigenous status: East Kimberley region,[c] 1981–2001

Year	Indigenous	Non-Indigenous	Total
1981	3,618	3,712	7,330
1986	4,175	4,525	8,700
1991	4,041	4,428	8,469
1996	4,877	4,507	9,394
2001	6,000	5,176	11,176

Notes: a. Indigenous and non-Indigenous estimates derived from total ERPs for the years 1981, 1986 and 1991

b. ABS generated Indigenous and non-Indigenous ERPs for 1996 and 2001

c. Wyndham-East Kimberley and Halls Creek SLAs

Figure 2.1. Indigenous and non-Indigenous estimated population levels: East Kimberley, 1981–2001

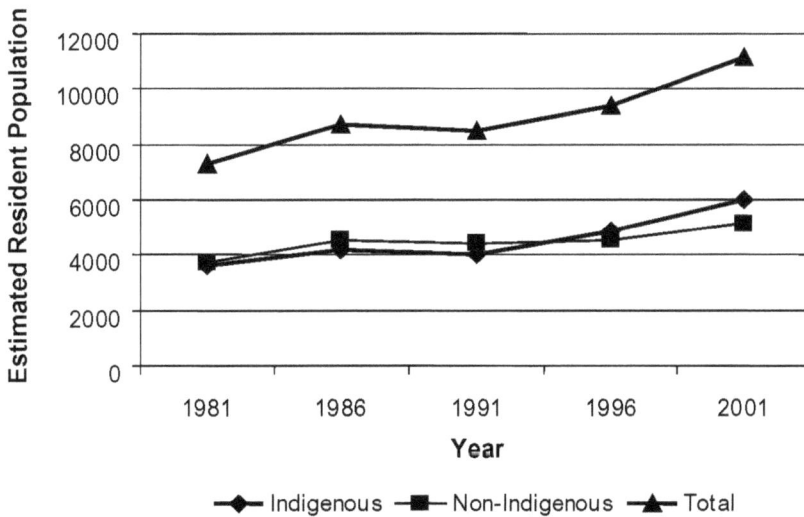

With the exception of 1991, this produces a curve of steady upward growth for both populations over the past 20 years. Of particular note is the fact that in 1996 the Indigenous population exceeded the non-Indigenous population (Figure 1). In 1981, the Indigenous share of the resident regional population was 49% and by 2001 it was 54%.

The study region

As a result of boundary changes over this period, what is less clear is how the balance of the estimated Indigenous and non-Indigenous populations within the Northern East Kimberley has shifted over time. An area approximating this region can be identified for 1981 using CDs, although usual residence counts were not available at this geographic level in 1981. Nonetheless, Indigenous and total place of enumeration counts are available at CD-level, and these can be used to begin to establish some sense of the population pattern. According to these figures, the Indigenous population counted within the study region (2,294) was only 36% of the total at that time. Of course, many of those counted were temporary visitors to the region, and the vast majority of these were non-Indigenous. If these are discounted, then the Indigenous share rises to 64.8%.

While it is difficult, in retrospect, to assess the quality of census counts in 1981, especially for the Indigenous population, at the very least an attempt can be made to adjust these counts to create 1981 population estimates benchmarked against the regional ERP, in much the same way as has been done for 2001 in Table 2.3. Such estimates for the Indigenous population within each component part of the study region[2] are shown in Table 2.4, along with calculations of the numeric and percentage change in population numbers to 2001.

Table 2.4. Indigenous derived ERPs for Indigenous Areas in the Northern East Kimberley, 1981 and 2001

Indigenous Area	Derived Indigenous ERP 1981	Derived Indigenous ERP 2001	Numeric change 1981–2001	% change 1981–2001	Annual % change
Kununurra	494	1,009	515	104.2	5.2
Wyndham	343	617	274	80.0	4.0
Oombulgurri	204	193	-9	-4.4	-0.2
Kalumburu	202	319	117	57.9	2.9
Lake Argyle	154	270	116	75.3	3.8
W/E-Kim (W)	40	169	129	322.5	16.1
Woolah	52	54	2	3.8	0.2
Warmun	217	324	107	49.3	2.5
Halls Creek	566	1,131	565	99.8	5.0
Halls Creek (N)	326	231	-95	-29.1	-1.4
Total region	2,599	4,317	1,718	66.1	3.3

A number of features emerge from these data. First, the overall annual growth rate of the Indigenous population in the Northern East Kimberley (3.3%) is slightly above what might have been expected due to natural increase. This suggests that some movement of Indigenous population into the area has occurred over the 20 year period. Second, there is considerable variation in growth between different localities and areas within the region.

On the whole, urban centres display the highest rates of growth, at levels pointing to net in-migration. Some communities appear to have remained more or less static in population size, suggesting net out-migration. In terms of redistribution, there appears to have been population loss in the southern part of the region, and population increase in the north-western area. However, this apparent loss in the south may simply reflect the relocation of people into places such as Warmun and Halls Creek.

Service populations

Mention has been made of the fact that a relatively large proportion of the population present in the East Kimberley at any one time is comprised of individuals whose usual place of residence is elsewhere. At the 2001 Census, just over 3,000 people, or 22% of the enumerated population in the East Kimberley, fell into this category. The vast majority of these, according to the census, were non-Indigenous people. Typically, in a region such as this, most such non-residents would be tourists and others would be temporary workers (Bell and Ward 2000). Some sense of the scale of such movement through the region is provided by data on estimated overnight visitor numbers in East Kimberley towns in 1994–95, with 70,000 reported in Kununurra, 47,000 in Wyndham, and 32,000 in Halls Creek (Kimberley Development Commission 1997: 36).

This addition to the resident population caused by the temporary movement of people into and out of the region is significant in remote areas such as the Kimberley as it more than offsets any population loss due to out-migration (Bell 2001: 13–14). It also adds to pressure on selected local services, whilst at the same time generating extra demand for goods and services and thereby enhancing regional economies of scale. To this extent, temporary migrants form an important element of the regional economy.

By their very nature, though, temporary movers are elusive in the context of formal statistical collection, and this is particularly the case among Indigenous populations in remote regions as they are frequently mobile over the short term (Taylor 1998). While this may lead to undercounting of the population at census time (Martin and Taylor 1996), it can also produce wide discrepancies between client-based population lists (for example, in the form of clinic registers) and official head counts.

For this reason, the Ord Valley Aboriginal Medical Service based in Kununurra maintains records of all its regular Aboriginal clients and it divides them into those who have a home address of Kununurra, and those whose address is via Kununurra, which essentially refers to surrounding (and distant) communities and outstations. In January 2003, the total numbers counted in this way amounted to 1,644 within Kununurra and 197 outside. It is interesting to compare at least the first of these figures with the derived Indigenous ERP for Kununurra of 1,009 as shown in Table 2.4. While direct comparison of these population levels is not possible owing to the different methods upon which they are based, the fact that the health service-based figure is almost two-thirds higher than the census-based estimate suggests that either the census-based estimate is too low, or that the health service-based figure includes individuals that the census might have counted as usual residents of places other than Kununurra. Resolution of such differences is no easy matter, and is beyond the scope of the present study. Suffice to say that such a variation underscores the fact that the numbers actually demanding and utilising services in the region may often exceed official estimates.

Population distribution

The nature and extent of Aboriginal participation in the regional economy can be greatly affected by the spatial distribution and residential structure of the population. One way of depicting this distribution has already been presented using IAs (Table 2.4) which shows that almost two-thirds of the Aboriginal population in the Northern East Kimberley (64%) is located in one of the three urban centres—an increase on the estimated 54% in 1981. This compares to 73% of the non-Indigenous population, a proportion that would be higher if those resident at the Argyle mine site were to be included. While there appears to have been a shift over time towards more urban residence, there is a problem in reading too much into this trend as the particular census geographic units employed here mask the considerable diversity of residential circumstances of Aboriginal people within the region.

Fortunately, the ABS has acquired a new means of representing Indigenous population distribution via the CHINS survey. This is rolled out ahead of the national census and includes an estimate of the resident population of all discrete Indigenous communities across the nation. According to the 2001 CHINS, a total of 55 discrete Aboriginal communities were located within the Northern East Kimberley with a collective estimated population of 2,879.[3] A number of these communities are town camps, some are larger service centres and townships, while most are outstations. Figure 2.2 shows the size of these settlements ranked in size order. There are five communities of between 200 and 450 persons (Kalumburu, Warmun, Oombulgurri, Mirima, and Mardiwa Loop). Below this are six communities of between 50 and 199 persons. At the bottom of the hierarchy is a long tail of some 44 very small communities of less than 50 persons.

Figure 2.2.   Rank size distribution of discrete Aboriginal communities in the Northern East Kimberley, 2001

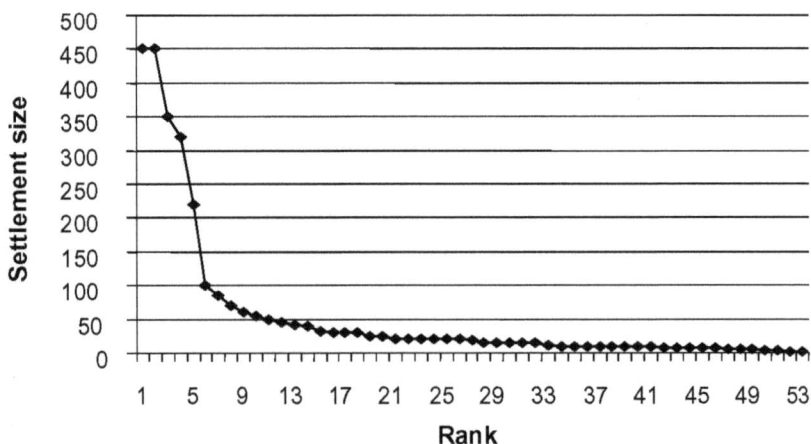

Source: ABS CHINS 2001 Confidentialised Unit Record File

These communities are distributed widely across the region, though with some clustering in and around Kununurra and Halls Creek, as well as close to other 'service' centres, such as Warmun, from which they represent an offshoot. This spatial fragmentation, borne of legal access to traditional lands, creates contrasting conditions for economic participation: on the one hand it presents a potential barrier to mainstream participation, while on the other hand it is a necessary feature of the customary economic sector.

Figure 2.3. **Distribution of discrete Indigenous communities in the Northern East Kimberley, 2001**

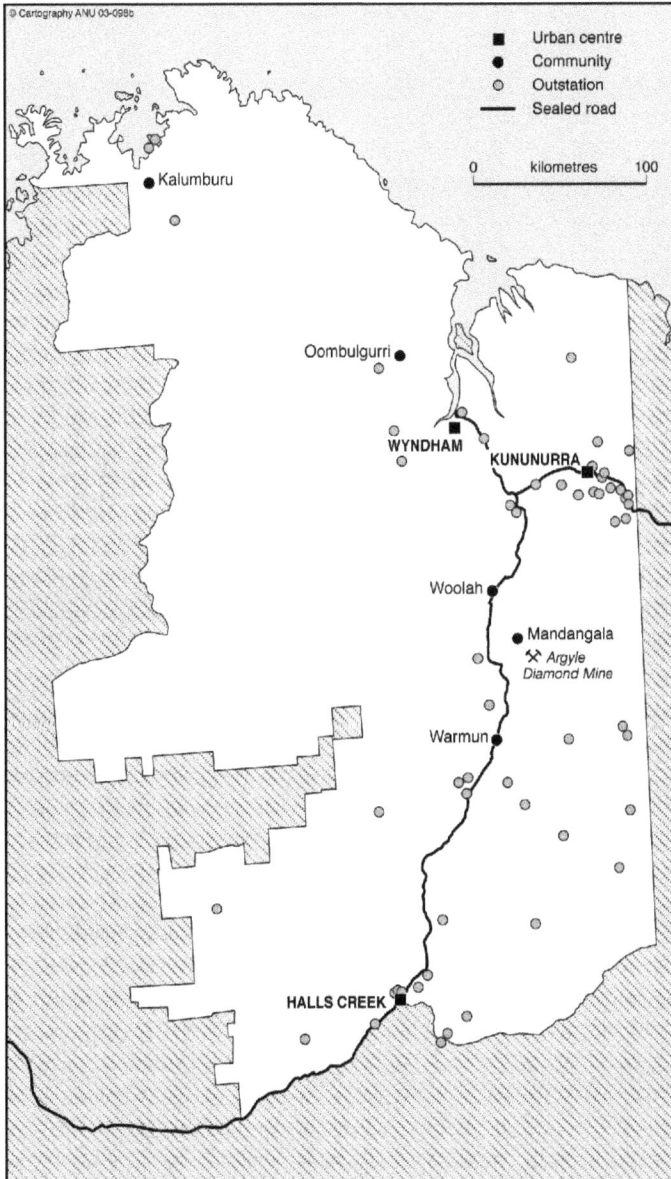

Age composition

A further demographic feature that has implications for current economic status and future economic need is the contrast between the age distribution of the Indigenous and non-Indigenous populations (as shown in Figure 2.4) for the East Kimberley region as a whole. For the Indigenous population, several features are noteworthy. First, the broad base of the age pyramid describes a population with continued high fertility (a Total Fertility Rate (TFR) of 3.3). Second, the rapid taper with advancing age highlights continued high adult mortality. Using the ABS experimental Indigenous life table for the Northern Territory (which arguably reflects age-specific mortality rates closest to those of the East Kimberley population), life expectancies for males and females are seemingly stuck at around 56 and 63 years respectively, with much of the excess mortality occurring in adult ages (ABS 2002b). Third, uniformity in the decline of population with age suggests net inter-regional migration balance. Finally, the relatively large numbers of women in the childbearing ages, and the even larger cohorts beneath them, indicate substantial population momentum with associated high potential for future growth in numbers. Actual numbers in each age group are shown for Indigenous males and females in Table 2.5.

Figure 2.4. **Distribution of the Indigenous and non-Indigenous populations[a] of the East Kimberley by age and sex, 2001**

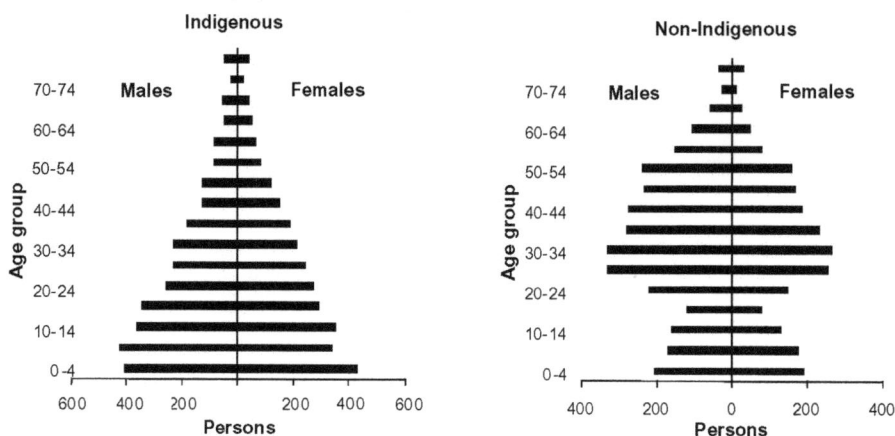

Note: a. Based on 2001 ABS ERP

By contrast, the non-Indigenous age distribution is typical of a population that is subject to selective inter-regional migration producing net gains among those of working age and their accompanying children, and net losses in the teen ages and at retirement. Underlying this pattern are high rates of population turnover (Taylor and Bell 1999). Furthermore, stability in the shape of the non-Indigenous age pyramid over time reflects the ongoing role of this region within the Western Australian economy as a place of selective migration tied to short-term employment opportunity (Bell and Maher 1995).

Table 2.5. Estimated Indigenous resident population by five year age group and sex: Northern East Kimberley, 2001

	Males	Females	Total
0-4	293	313	606
5-9	303	250	553
10-14	260	256	516
15-19	246	212	458
20-24	183	202	385
25-29	168	178	345
30-34	167	158	325
35-39	132	141	273
40-44	91	112	202
45-49	89	89	178
50-54	58	62	120
55-59	58	50	107
60-64	35	42	78
65-69	36	31	67
70-74	14	22	36
75+	35	33	68
Total	2,166	2,151	4,317

The study region

For the population in the study region, place of enumeration data are utilised to examine whether any variation is evident in the age distribution of those Indigenous people counted in the three towns of Kununurra, Wyndham and Halls Creek as opposed to those counted in rural communities. The idea here is that the towns may be more attractive to certain age groups since they contain high schools and post-secondary training facilities, and are the focus of most mainstream employment in the region. Table 2.6 examines this proposition for Aboriginal residents of the region and the data show very little variation between town and country populations. If anything, the age profile in towns is slightly older, especially among females, but the proportion of the population in the young adult age group of 15-24 is lower in towns than in communities. In both sets of locations, the age pattern is very similar to that described by the ERP for the East Kimberley as a whole, with around 40% of the population under 15 years of age and very low proportions of people over 65 years.

Table 2.6. Percentage age distribution of the Indigenous population counted in communities and towns within the Northern East Kimberley, 2001

	Communities			Towns		
	Males	Females	Total	Males	Females	Total
0-4	12.8	15.5	14.1	15.0	14.2	14.5
5-14	25.3	24.9	25.1	26.2	21.8	23.8
15-24	22.0	19.8	21.0	16.8	18.4	17.6
25-44	26.3	24.3	25.4	24.8	29.9	27.5
45-64	9.8	10.5	10.1	13.1	11.6	12.3
65+	3.8	5.0	4.4	4.2	4.2	4.2
Total	100.0	100.0	100.0	100.0	100.0	100.0

Source: Indigenous Area Profiles, ABS Cat. no. 2002.0

Population projections

To date, planning processes in Indigenous communities have all too often relied on dated demographic information. This creates a sense of uncertainty in assessing the adequacy of policy to address shortfalls in social and economic infrastructure. Such policy development is typically reactive to needs as they become evident (for example, in terms of post facto responses to housing shortages), as opposed to being proactive in seeking to anticipate and plan for expected requirements. However, being proactive requires a measure of future requirements for government works and services, and this is something that is only rarely achieved for Indigenous communities. This is not the case for mainstream communities throughout Australia where the approach to settlement planning is much more prospective.

For example, State and local government planning authorities routinely develop future scenarios and often seek budgetary allocations on the basis of anticipated needs. A key element in this process is the production of small-area population projections or forecasts. While the ABS provides official projections of State and Territory and SLA populations, the individual States and Territories, in turn, also produce regional and local area projections, often down to the Local Government Area level (Bell 1992; W.A. Ministry of Planning 2000). For these purposes a standard cohort-component methodology is generally applied, and this practice is adopted here to project the Indigenous population of the East Kimberley as a whole to 2016. Future population numbers in the study region are then derived pro rata.

Projection assumptions

The cohort-component method carries forward the preliminary 2001 Indigenous ERP for the East Kimberley to 2016 by successive five-year periods. The projection is based on ageing the population by five-year blocks, subjecting each group to age- and sex-specific mortality, fertility and net migration regimes as follows:

- Survival rates from the Indigenous life tables for the Northern Territory (ABS 2002b) are applied on the assumption that these are more likely to reflect the mortality profile of Indigenous people in the study region than rates derived from the Western Australian life table. These rates are also held constant for the projection period because evidence shows that life expectancy generally for Indigenous people in recent times has shown no sign of improvement (Kinfu and Taylor 2002).

- Age specific fertility rates based on births to Indigenous women in the Western Australian Midwives Notification System for the SLAs of Wyndham-East Kimberley and Halls Creek are applied. These data produce a TFR of 3.3, which is substantially higher than the Indigenous TFR of 2.2 for Western Australia as a whole and is more in line with rates reported from similar remote regions of Northern Australia (Taylor & Bell 2001).

- In the absence of an operational model of migration, and in light of the erratic pattern displayed by net migration estimates (Taylor & Bell 2001), net migration is held at zero for all ages.

- No allowance is made for population change via shifts in Indigenous identification.

Projection results

The actual projection is conducted separately for males and females in five-year blocks from 2001 to 2016. Projected births for the 2001-2006 period are added to the existing 2001 population (see Table 2.5) and each cohort is then subjected to respective survival rates to arrive at an estimate of the population in each age group in 2006. This process is continued through to 2016.

Projections of the non-Indigenous population are more problematic. One approach to developing these might be to derive them as a residual between the Indigenous projections and projections of the total regional population. Projections for the total population were produced by the Western Australian Ministry of Planning using 1996 ERPs as the base, but at the time of writing 2001-based projections had not been prepared. However, given that the assumptions underlying the development of estimates for the Indigenous and total populations are inevitably quite different, the creation of a residual (non-Indigenous) population in this way is statistically problematic. Any estimation and projection of a 'non-Indigenous' population would need to be guided by its own unique underlying assumptions, and the development of these is beyond the scope of the present exercise. Indeed, the social construction of such a population raises questions as to whether it is statistically possible at all. For these reasons, projections of the non-Indigenous population are not presented here.

Table 2.7.   Indigenous population of the East Kimberley Region by five year age group: 2001 and 2016

Age group	ERP 2001	Projection 2016	Net change	% change
0-4	842	1,089	247	29.3
5-9	769	986	217	28.2
10-14	717	893	176	24.5
15-19	637	837	200	31.4
20-24	535	755	220	41.1
25-29	480	694	214	44.6
30-34	452	604	152	33.6
35-39	379	498	119	31.4
40-44	281	433	152	54.1
45-49	247	385	138	55.9
50-54	167	310	143	85.6
55-59	149	218	69	46.3
60-64	108	174	66	61.1
65-69	93	103	10	10.8
70-74	50	74	24	48.0
75+	94	44	-50	-53.2
Total	6,000	8,098	2,098	35.0

Indigenous population totals projected to 2016 for the East Kimberley region are shown in Table 2.7 by five year age group, together with numeric and percentage change from the 2001 ERP. Overall, by 2016, the Indigenous population is projected to increase by 35% (or 2.3% per annum) to reach a population of 8,098, an increase of just over 2,000 persons. If the Northern East Kimberley retains its 2001 share of this wider regional population (72%), then the projected Indigenous population of the study region in 2016 will be 5,831 (an increase of 1,514). As shown by the percentage change by age group, much of this growth will occur in the working age groups with the population aged between 15 and 50 years increasing by some 1,338. Once again, if the Northern East Kimberley share remains the same, then numbers in this working age range will increase by around 1,000.

While this projection is correct according to the algorithms applied, it is only preliminary and there are several refinements that, if developed, would provide for greater certainty in the assumptions. In particular, there may be scope for some refinement of net migration assumptions based on a greater appreciation of regional economic development plans, especially in regard to Indigenous employment targets, and other social and economic factors that may induce migration. An allied issue here would be the need for more detailed analysis of inter-regional population movement for education and training purposes.

One device frequently deployed to canvass a range of possible projection outcomes is the calculation of several projection series based on varying assumptions. The current calculations involve the use of only one series. An obvious option, then, for further development of these projections would be to generate alternative scenarios based on possible combinations of falling/rising/stable fertility and mortality and varying assumptions about net migration. While there is some heuristic potential here, it obviously makes sense to base such exploration on plausible indicators, and so the indicators themselves would also need to be assessed.

In using the projections as a means of targeting policy, it is possible to estimate the future size of the Indigenous and non-Indigenous resident labour force by applying labour force participation rates to the projected working-age populations. If likely future trends in employment numbers could also be established, then the quantum of need for additional job creation may be calculated according to specified or agreed employment levels. This exercise would essentially represent a regionalised version of similar calculations of Indigenous employment demand made at the national level (Taylor and Hunter 1998; Hunter, Kinfu and Taylor 2003).

Notes

1. Discrete communities are defined by the ABS as geographic locations that are bounded by physical or cadastral boundaries, and inhabited or intended to be inhabited predominantly by Indigenous people (more than 50 per cent), with housing and infrastructure that is either owned or managed on a community basis (ABS, 2000: 66).

2. This same calculation cannot be made for the non-Indigenous population at the Indigenous Area level, or for the study region as a whole, owing to the large proportion of non-usual residents in the non-Indigenous place of enumeration count.

3. This CHINS reports estimates of the usual resident population of each community based on information provided to survey collectors by key informants in community housing organisations, councils and resource centres.

3. Aboriginal participation in the regional labour market

As with most Aboriginal settlements in north Australia, those in the Northern East Kimberley were established without a modern economic base, and have not subsequently acquired one, at least not in a manner that is currently sustainable beyond the provisions of the welfare state. Basically, the shift out of pastoral employment a generation ago has yet to be replaced with any firm engagement by local Aboriginal people in the emergent regional labour market which is dominated by employment in irrigated agriculture, mining, tourism, and the provision of government services.

While it is true that the overall employment rate for Aboriginal people in the East Kimberley as a whole has risen since 1981 from around 39% of all adults to 46%, net gains in employment over this period have been due entirely to the expansion of CDEP scheme activities. This is underlined by the fact that the employment rate net of CDEP—what can be described as the mainstream employment rate—actually fell from 39% to only 16%. To be fair, some of this decline reflects the substitution effect of CDEP, with many jobs that might otherwise be classified as part of the mainstream labour market (especially in the provision of local government-type services) being absorbed by the scheme.

In effect, though, the decline in the Aboriginal mainstream employment rate serves to emphasise the rise to dominance of CDEP in the regional Aboriginal labour market. In 1981, there were no CDEP schemes in the East Kimberley, and the 750 Aboriginal people recorded in employment were therefore in the mainstream labour market. By the time of the 2001 Census, there were 7 CDEP schemes in the study region with 838 participants, but only 428 Aboriginal people in the mainstream workforce. Over the same period, mainstream employment among non-Aboriginal residents of the region increased by 32%, while employment at Argyle for non-residents via fly-in fly-out also grew. Census data on industry of employment for non-Aboriginal usual residents of the region suggest that 103 (20%) of the 525 non-Aboriginal workers at the mine site in 2001 were drawn from local sources.

While the regional labour market has grown in both size and complexity, Aboriginal participation has receded. In effect, the past 30 years have witnessed a simple shift from an historical Aboriginal association with private sector employment in the form of the pastoral industry, to an association with the government sector in the form of CDEP. Beyond this, as noted, only 16% of Aboriginal adults now participate in the mainstream labour market compared to 82% of non-Aboriginal residents. This structural gap in employment, together with low levels of Aboriginal labour force participation, has significant consequences for current Aboriginal economic status, as well as for consideration of future options regarding Aboriginal participation in the regional economy.

There are three reasons for this. First of all, regardless of whatever targets might be met in respect of local employment at Argyle mine, the major regional impacts on Aboriginal people in terms of raising their overall labour force and economic status are likely to depend more on administrative and funding decisions regarding CDEP than anything else. Thus, future growth of the scheme is dependent on ever expanding resources from government, while the current welfare basis for CDEP funding leaves little scope for advancing employment beyond part-time hours with corresponding low income return.

Second, CDEP would inevitably form part of any comprehensive planning for regional economic development focused on future activities at Argyle mine. This is because much of the locally based potential workforce for the mine would in all likelihood be currently engaged by a CDEP scheme and be building necessary skills and experience via such employment. Also, many of the regional multipliers from Argyle in the form of enterprise development are likely to accrue to CDEP schemes given their predominant role in pursuing such opportunities.

Finally, the extent of reliance on CDEP for generating employment opportunities in the region places a premium on the local workforce targets of Argyle as the main opportunity in the foreseeable future for creating and hopefully sustaining at least some growth in Aboriginal mainstream employment. To date, the indications that ADM's apparently ambitious targets might be met have been encouraging. What remains unclear, though, is whether there will be any discernable impact on regional labour force and economic indicators if such targets are met. The essential background to considering this question is one of high projected growth in the Aboriginal working age population set against future job needs and likely employment outcomes.

Regional labour force status

Rates of labour force status and estimated levels are shown for Aboriginal and non-Aboriginal residents of the study region in Table 3.1. Three standard indicators of labour force status are established:

1. the *employment/population ratio*, representing the percentage of persons aged 15 years and over who indicated in the census that they were in employment (either in CDEP or in mainstream work) during the week prior to enumeration;

2. the *unemployment rate*, expressing those who indicated that they were not in employment but had actively looked for work during the four weeks prior to enumeration, as a percentage of those aged 15 years and over;

3. the *labour force participation rate*, representing persons in the labour force (employed and unemployed) as a percentage of those of working age.

Table 3.1. Labour force status rates[a] and estimated levels for Aboriginal and non-Aboriginal residents of the Northern East Kimberley, 2001

	Employed		Unemployed	Not in the labour force	Total 15+
	CDEP	Mainstream			
	Levels				
Aboriginal	779	428	132	1,302	2,641
Non-Aboriginal	55	3,222	83	614	3,974
	Rates				
Aboriginal	29.5	16.2	5.0	49.3	100.0
Non-Aboriginal	1.4	81.3	2.1	15.5	100.0

Note: a. Excludes labour force status not stated

Source: ABS 2001 Census of Population and Housing, customised tables

Overall, the size of the regional labour force (all residents employed in CDEP and mainstream work plus those unemployed) amounts to 4,699. However, with almost half (1,302) of all Aboriginal adults not in the labour force (according to the census definition), as much as 71% of the resident regional labour force is non-Aboriginal. Some of the estimated levels of Aboriginal labour force status have caveats attached. First of all, the 779 indicated by ABS statistics in CDEP employment is somewhat lower than the 838 Aboriginal participants in the scheme recorded by ATSIC at the same time as the 2001 Census. This variation may reflect the fact that the census records employment in the 'last' week, while CDEP work is intermittent and predominantly part-time. It may also reflect residual census undercount not accounted for by the estimation of employment levels. Also noticeable is that the census-recorded unemployment rate appears very low when set against the 600 Aboriginal clients of Centrelink who were in receipt of Newstart Allowance at the time of the 2001 Census. However, many of these are exempt from activity testing and may well have been recorded under CDEP or not in the labour force in census data. Indeed, given the administratively determined nature of much Aboriginal economic activity in the region, the boundaries between officially recorded employment, unemployment, and consequent labour force participation rates, are sufficiently blurred that all these data should be approached with some caution. They are best seen as rough estimates rather than as robust indicators.

Of particular interest for social impact planning is the distribution of employment and related labour force status by age. This is shown in Figure 3.1 for Aboriginal residents of the Northern East Kimberley with the actual rates provided in Table 3.2. The most striking feature is the fact that participation in CDEP is higher than participation in mainstream employment among youth and those of younger working age between 15 and 44 years. Only in the 45-54 age group does mainstream employment outstrip CDEP. As expected, labour force participation is positively correlated with age up to 44 years, but recedes rapidly thereafter, indicating a distinctly shortened working-life span. One prospect is that this reflects increased morbidity with advancing age, a proposition that will be tested later with hospital separations data. Thus, those most active in the labour market are generally under 45 years of age. To the extent that local recruitment for the mine workforce over the proposed extended life of Argyle mine is likely to be drawn from those aged 15-34 years in 2001, these data suggest that relatively few (an estimated 253) have experience in mainstream work, with the majority (507) in CDEP.

Figure 3.1. Labour force status rates by age group: Aboriginal residents of the Northern East Kimberley, 2001

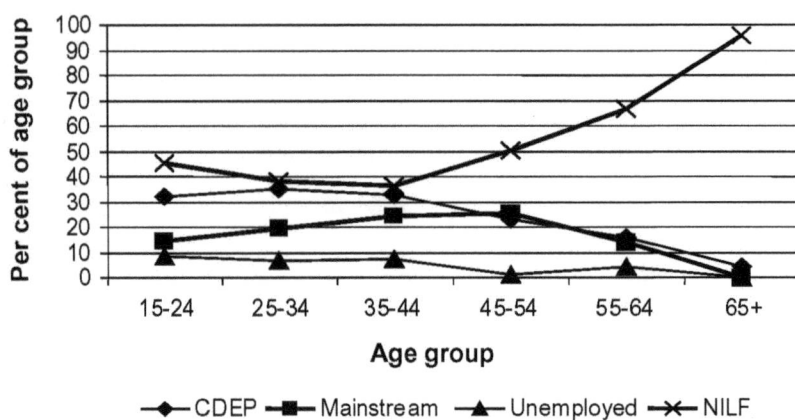

Table 3.2. Labour force status rates by age group: Aboriginal residents of the Northern East Kimberley, 2001

	CDEP	Mainstream	Unemployed	NILF	Total
15-24	32.1	14.3	8.4	45.2	100.0
25-34	35.3	19.7	6.7	38.3	100.0
35-44	32.5	24.0	7.0	36.5	100.0
45-54	23.1	25.5	1.2	50.2	100.0
55-64	15.8	13.8	3.9	66.5	100.0
65+	4.1	0.0	0.0	95.9	100.0

Source: ABS 2001 Census of Population and Housing, customised tables

Dependency ratios

Measures of the potential economic implications of a given age structure can be combined with data on labour force status to produce a range of dependency ratios. These are shown in Table 3.3 for the Aboriginal population of the Northern East Kimberley in 2001, with comparison drawn from Western Australia as a whole. The *childhood dependency* ratio is the simplest of these measures and expresses the number of children in the population (aged 0-14 years) as a ratio of the working-age population (defined here as aged 15-55, given the significance of adult morbidity). Obviously, a ratio of 1.0 would indicate that the size of the two age groups is the same and that there is one person of working age for every child. A figure greater than 1.0 indicates more than one child to each person of working age, and less than 1.0 indicates less than one child to each person of working age. Obviously, this only provides an indication of the ratio of potential economic providers to dependents, as it takes no account of the economically inactive.

Table 3.3.   Dependency ratios for the Aboriginal populations of the Northern East Kimberley and Western Australia, 2001

Dependency ratio	Northern East Kimberley	Western Australia
Childhood dependency	0.7	0.7
Childhood burden	1.3	1.6
Childhood burden (excl. CDEP)	3.9	2.3
Dependency ratio	2.7	2.2
Economic burden	2.6	2.9
Economic burden (excl. CDEP)	9.1	4.8

Source: ABS 2001 Census of Population and Housing, customised tables and ABS cat no.

In the study region, the *childhood dependency* ratio was 0.73 which is similar to the 0.72 reported for Aboriginal people generally in Western Australia. In effect, there are 0.7 Aboriginal children to each Aboriginal adult of working age. While this may appear to be a favourable ratio at one level, it represents far more children per adult compared to the ratio of 0.29 recorded for the non-Aboriginal population of the region.

More refined measures of dependency incorporate some indication of the ability of working-age adults to support others. The *childhood burden*, for example, is defined as the ratio of the number of children to the number of employed persons. Once again, a figure of 1.0 indicates parity. According to census-based estimates, there were 1.3 Aboriginal children to each employed adult if all those engaged by the CDEP scheme are considered to be in employment. If, however, this calculation is based on those employed only in non-CDEP work, then the ratio is much higher at 3.9. The fact that the equivalent ratio for all Aboriginal people in Western Australia is much lower at 2.3 underlines the considerable reliance on CDEP in the study region as the primary support mechanism for large numbers of child dependents.

Another measure is provided by the *dependency ratio* which represents the ratio of children and economically inactive adults to the labour force (those employed plus those unemployed). This produces an average of 2.7 dependents per economically active person, but if the focus were solely on those in mainstream employment the dependency ratio would be much higher.

Finally, the *economic burden* is a ratio of the number of children and economically inactive persons (including here those unemployed) to employed persons. This shows that for each employed Aboriginal person (including those in the CDEP scheme) there are 2.6 other Aboriginal people who are not employed, a figure similar to the state average. If, however, those in CDEP are excluded from the economically active then the economic burden in the study region is almost double the state average at 9.1 dependents per income earner.

From a regional planning perspective, then, the youthful Aboriginal age profile is a key demographic feature when set against the relatively poor labour force status of adults. In effect, there are 9 dependents, on average, for each Aboriginal employee in the mainstream labour market. This represents a notably higher economic burden for the regional Aboriginal population than recorded for the Aboriginal population generally in Western Australia. However, perhaps of more significance in the local context of access to resources and consumer spending, is the fact that the burden is massively higher than observed among non-Aboriginal residents of the region (0.5 dependents per income earner) with whom Aboriginal residents can draw direct comparison.

Industry and occupation

In the final analysis, employment is a means to personal income generation, while the amount generated is determined largely by occupational status. In turn, the availability of particular occupations within a region is partly related to the industry mix of economic activities. Thus, the relative distribution of Aboriginal and non-Aboriginal employment by industry and occupational category is a vital feature of participation in the regional labour market and this is shown in Figures 3.2 and 3.3 for male and female workers respectively.

Figure 3.2.   Distribution of resident Aboriginal and non-Aboriginal male employment by industry division: Northern East Kimberley, 2001

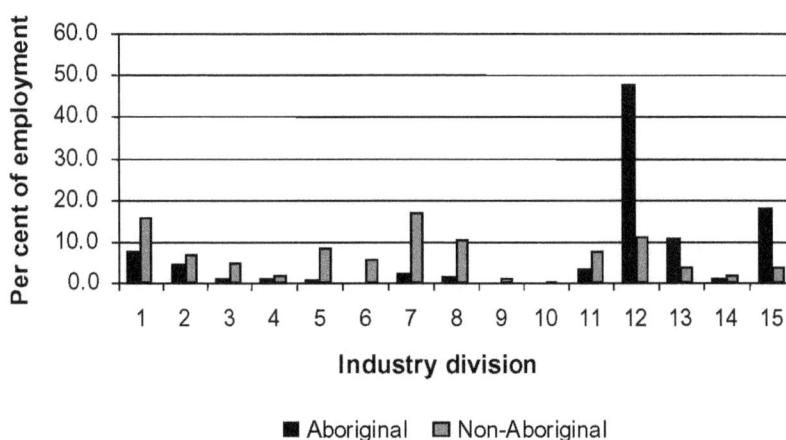

Key: 1. Agriculture, Forestry and Fishing. 2. Mining. 3. Manufacturing. 4. Electricity, Gas and Water Supply. 5. Construction. 6. Wholesale Trade. 7. Retail Trade. 8. Transport and Storage. 9. Communication Services. 10. Finance and Insurance. 11. Property and Business Services. 12. Government Administration and Defence. 13. Health and Community Services. 14. Cultural and Recreational Services. 15. Personal and Other Services.

Figure 3.3. Distribution of resident Aboriginal and non-Aboriginal female employment by industry division: Northern East Kimberley, 2001

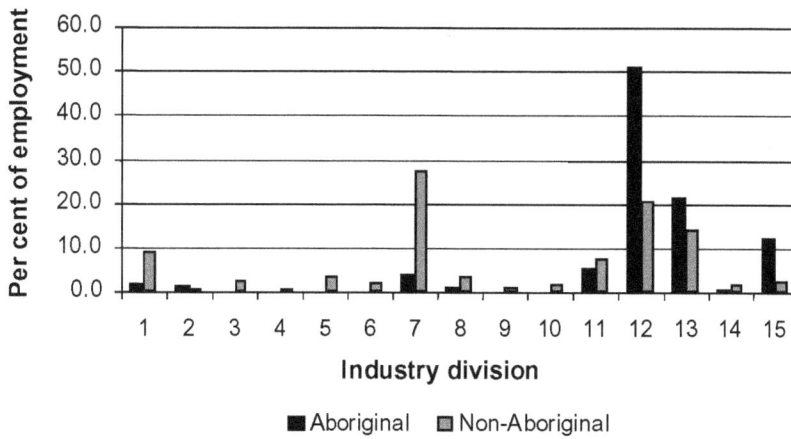

Key: 1.Agriculture, Forestry and Fishing. 2.Mining. 3.Manufacturing. 4.Electricity, Gas and Water Supply. 5.Construction. 6.Wholesale Trade. 7.Retail Trade. 8.Transport and Storage. 9.Communication Services. 10.Finance and Insurance. 11.Property and Business Services. 12.Government Administration and Defence. 13.Health and Community Services. 14.Cultural and Recreational Services. 15.Personal and Other Services.

Clearly, the distribution of Aboriginal employment by industry division for both males and females is quite different from that of their respective non-Aboriginal counterparts. Aboriginal employment is heavily concentrated in government administration, which in effect reflects the census classification of much CDEP employment. Another focus for both Aboriginal males and females is in health and community services and personal service industries, while agriculture (the pastoral industry) also appears as a relatively prominent employer of Aboriginal male labour. Overall, though, there is little difference in industry distribution between Aboriginal males and females, as indicated by an index of dissimilarity of only 17.8 (see endnote for explanation).[1]

However, the same cannot be said for the comparison of Aboriginal and non-Aboriginal industry distribution. Clearly, the non-Aboriginal workforce is more widely spread across a range of industry categories with some emphasis on agriculture, construction, retailing, and transport among males, and on agriculture, retailing, government administration and health and community services among females. Of interest is the fact that mining represents a relatively small employer of the locally resident non-Aboriginal workforce. If non-resident workers were included as part of the make up of the regional labour market then the mining sector would dominate the overall profile with a total of 573 full-time equivalent workers on site at Argyle alone in 2001.

The actual scale of difference between the percentage representation of Aboriginal and non-Aboriginal workers in each industry division is shown in Table 3.4 with negative signs indicating those industries where Aboriginal workers are under-represented compared to non-Aboriginal workers. Clearly, the retail industry stands out in this regard for both males and females, followed by agriculture, construction and transport and storage industries.

The overwhelming representation of Aboriginal workers in government administration, and to a lesser extent in health and community services, is also highlighted. These variations contribute to relatively high indices of dissimilarity, especially for males. In short, if the Aboriginal workforce were to participate in the industry mix of the regional labour market in the same fashion as non-Aboriginal workers, then according to the index of dissimilarity more than half of them (53.3%) would need to change their industry of employment. Obviously, this would represent a substantial restructure.

Table 3.4.   Differentials in employment distribution between Aboriginal and non-Aboriginal workers by industry division: Northern East Kimberley, 2001

Industry division	Difference in per cent employed		
	Males	Females	Total
Agriculture, Forestry and Fishing	-7.8	-7.0	-7.3
Mining	-2.5	0.8	-1.0
Manufacturing	-3.7	-2.6	-3.1
Electricity, Gas and Water Supply	-0.6	-0.7	-0.5
Construction	-7.7	-3.4	-5.8
Wholesale Trade	-5.9	-2.3	-4.4
Retail Trade	-14.5	-23.8	-18.6
Transport and Storage	-8.6	-2.6	-5.8
Communication Services	-1.2	-1.2	-1.3
Finance and Insurance	-0.3	-1.9	-1.0
Property and Business Services	-4.1	-2.3	-3.6
Government Administration and Defence	36.6	30.9	34.2
Health and Community Services	6.8	7.3	6.7
Cultural and Recreational Services	-0.6	-1.1	-0.9
Personal and Other Services	14.1	9.9	12.4
Index of dissimilarity	57.5	48.9	53.3

A similar scale of difference in workforce participation is evident in respect of occupational distributions (Figures 3.4 and 3.5). Much of this arises from the ABS tendency to code CDEP scheme workers as labourers and related workers. As a consequence, more than 60% of Aboriginal male workers, and almost 40% of female workers are classified in this way. By contrast, non-Aboriginal workers are more evenly distributed across occupational groups, especially in the more skilled occupations in categories 1-4. There is evidence, however, that Aboriginal female workers gravitate to similar occupations as their non-Aboriginal counterparts, especially as intermediate clerical, sales and service workers. This is reflected in a lower index of dissimilarity between female workers compared to male, while the index between Aboriginal male and female workers (35.6) is also considerably higher than recorded for industry divisions (Table 3.5). Overall, though, Aboriginal workers are substantially under-represented in the more skilled occupations, especially males, and more than 40% would need to shift their occupational group if they were to match the skill set of the regional non-Aboriginal workforce.

Figure 3.4.   **Distribution of resident Aboriginal and non-Aboriginal male employment by occupational group: Northern East Kimberley, 2001**

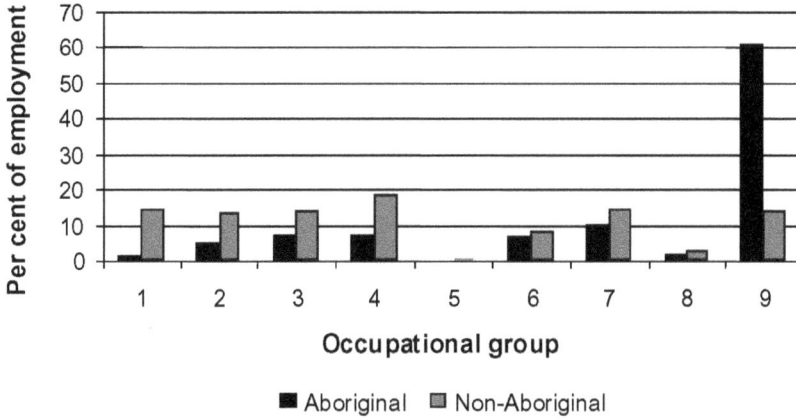

Key: 1.Managers and Administrators. 2.Professionals. 3.Associate Professionals. 4.Tradespersons and Related Workers. 5. Advanced Clerical and Service Workers. 6. Intermediate Clerical, Sales and Service Workers. 7. Intermediate Production and Transport Workers. 8.Elementary Clerical, Sales and Service Workers. 9.Labourers and Related Workers.

Figure 3.5.   **Distribution of resident Aboriginal and non-Aboriginal female employment by occupational group: Northern East Kimberley, 2001**

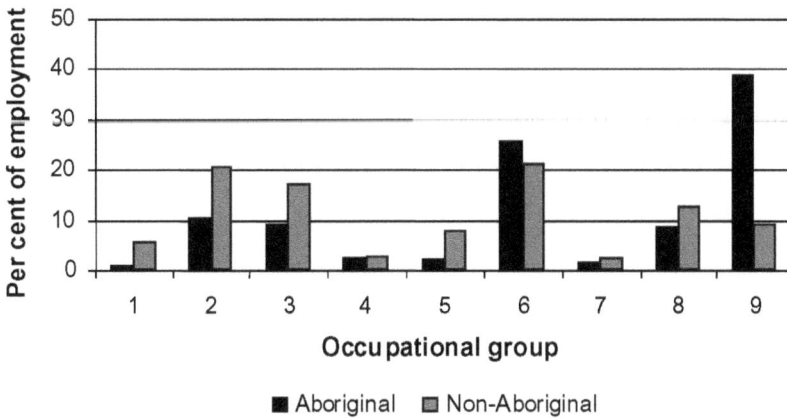

Key: 1.Managers and Administrators. 2.Professionals. 3.Associate Professionals. 4.Tradespersons and Related Workers. 5. Advanced Clerical and Service Workers. 6. Intermediate Clerical, Sales and Service Workers. 7. Intermediate Production and Transport Workers. 8. Elementary Clerical, Sales and Service Workers. 9.Labourers and Related Workers.

Table 3.5. **Differentials in employment distribution between Aboriginal and non-Aboriginal workers by occupational group: Northern East Kimberley, 2001**

Occupational group	Difference in per cent employed		
	Males	Females	Total
Managers and Administrators	-13.2	-4.8	-9.8
Professionals	-8.4	-10.2	-9.0
Associate Professionals	-7.0	-7.9	-7.3
Tradespersons and Related Workers	-11.6	-0.6	-7.1
Advanced Clerical and Service Workers	-0.4	-5.9	-2.6
Intermediate Clerical, Sales and Service Workers	-1.3	4.6	1.3
Intermediate Production and Transport Workers	-4.9	-0.9	-3.3
Elementary Clerical, Sales and Service Workers	-0.7	-4.2	-2.0
Labourers and Related Workers	47.5	29.7	40.0
Index of dissimilarity	47.5	34.4	41.2

CDEP activities

One drawback of census-derived industry and occupational data is their tendency to apply blanket classification to CDEP scheme employment. As shown above, this results in a high concentration of Aboriginal employment in government administration (especially local government) and as labourers. It is also the case that because of the employment substitution effect of CDEP, much work classified as CDEP actually covers a wider range of industry and employment categories than is apparent from census coding. An example here would be CDEP work in an aquaculture project. If this were in the mainstream labour market it would be classified under agriculture, fishing and forestry as an industry, and the workers may well be classified as farm hands or skilled agricultural workers depending on the nature of the job. Instead, the tendency is for them to be classified as labourers in local government.

The argument here is that census coding of CDEP masks a good deal of diversity in the pattern of Aboriginal participation in the regional economy. One way to demonstrate this is to use information from the activity worksheets of CDEP schemes that provide details of individual economic activities. Among those listed within the region in 2003 are:

> grading, fencing, road maintenance, plant maintenance and operation, manufacture of canvas products, manufacture of jewelry, school of the air, media, landscaping, sewing, house and other building construction, non-building construction, plumbing and electrical maintenance, pipe laying, painting and decorating, visual arts, ceramics, screen printing, market gardening, livestock management, pastoral work, rodeo horse training, vehicle repair, aquaculture, youth and men's support activities, Centrelink

services, clinic assistants, teachers assistants, sport and recreation activities, office assistants, store assistants, police wardens, fruit growing, contract chipping of green waste, and retailing.

Given the key role played by CDEP in terms of providing for Aboriginal employment in the region there is a need to fully acknowledge this diversity of economic activity and to explore ways in which vital elements might articulate with Argyle and other regionally-based developments either via direct contracting, sub-contracting and/or joint venturing.

Argyle mine employment: history and future targets

For the most part, since the commencement of mining at Argyle, Aboriginal employment has comprised only a small fraction of the total (Figures 3.6 and 3.7). From the first intake of 14 Aboriginal workers in 1985, accounting for 2.5% of the workforce, the number of Aboriginal people employed on-site at Argyle, and their proportional share of total on-site employment, rose to an initial peak in the early 1990s, only to fall away again to relatively low levels by the end of the 1990s. However, since 1999, with the introduction of company plans to enhance Aboriginal employment at the mine, the numbers have steadily increased with an initial ADM target of having Aboriginal employees comprise 15% of the total by 2005 already exceeded by the end of 2003. In November 2003, the overall mine workforce had increased to 687, and fully 125 (18%) of these were Aboriginal (Figures 3.6 and 3.7). Part of this increase in both overall and Aboriginal numbers reflects the increased use of contracted labour from labour hire companies within the East Kimberley. At the end of 2003, a total of 101 on-site workers (including some trainees) were sourced from Kimberley Crane Hire, Kimberley Group Training, and Countryman Hire. All of these are hired locally, and one-third (34) were Aboriginal people. Presently, 61% of ADM employees at Argyle mine are fly-in/fly-out (FI/FO) workers and these are almost all non-Aboriginal.

This current situation represents the high watermark of Argyle operations over the past two decades in terms of workforce size and composition. Depending on the decision (due in 2005) to either proceed with the proposed underground mining operation, or to forgo this option and wind down pit production in 2007, finish processing in 2010, and then decommission the mine, future operations will look very different to those of the past 20 years. If underground mining proceeds, this will involve overlapping construction phases leading to underground production alongside an extension of pit operations. It will involve a rapid winding back of the FI/FO workforce to just 20% with the bulk of the workforce sourced locally from within the East Kimberley region (defined in wider terms than just the Northern East Kimberley as it is based on a radius of reasonable weekly roster commuting time and therefore extends to the area south of Halls Creek and as far west as Fitzroy Crossing). Within this restructuring plan, ADM aims to ensure that at least 50% of this locally-recruited workforce is made up of Aboriginal people.

Figure 3.6. Aboriginal and total employment at Argyle Diamond Mine: 1983–2003

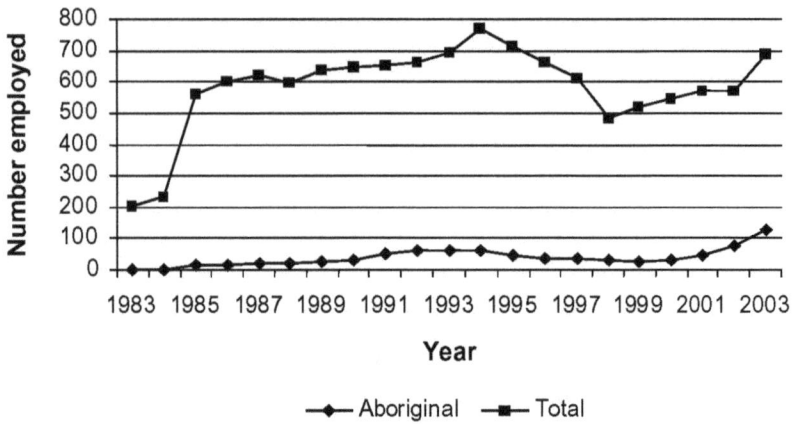

Source: ADM Community Relations and Regional Business Development Units

Figure 3.7. Aboriginal percentage of total Argyle mine workforce: 1983–2003

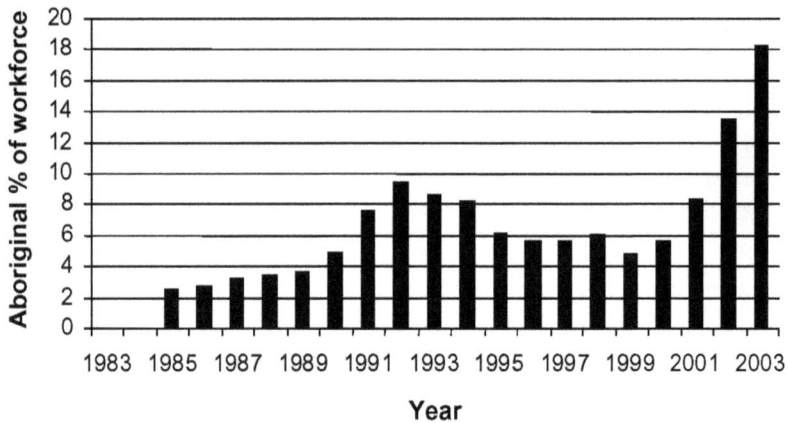

Source: ADM Community Relations and Regional Business Development Units

As for the current ratio of local to non-local workers, in late 2001 the ADM Community Relations department conducted a survey of its Aboriginal mine workforce and determined that 71% were local workers from within the Northern East Kimberley region (20% from Wyndham, 25% from Kununurra, 21% from Halls Creek, 3% from Warmun, and 3% from Wuggabin). The remaining 29% were from the West Kimberley and Perth. Thus, at the time of the 2001 Census, total Aboriginal employment at the mine site was 48, and from the above ratio 34 of these can be estimated to have been locally sourced (Table 3.6). In line with company efforts to recruit locally, by November of 2003 the ratio of local to non-local Aboriginal workers had risen from 71% to 95% (Table 3.6).

Table 3.6.   Summary of ADM employment mix 1985–2003

	Total ADM employees	Indigenous ADM employees	Indigenous employees as % of total	Indigenous employees sourced locally	Ratio of local/ non-local Indigenous employees
1985	560	14	2.5	?	?
2001	573	48	8.4	34	0.71
2003	687	125	18.2	119	0.95

Source: ADM Community Relations and Regional Business Development Units

The current mine workforce can be divided into four broad activity areas: asset management, production mining, production processing, and miscellaneous operational support areas such as security, health and safety, planning, and training (Table 3.7). Almost half of all Aboriginal employees (excluding contracted labour) are in production mining jobs, especially in loading and hauling. The remainder are scattered across the employment spectrum, though with some emphasis on asset management jobs such as maintenance. This focus on loading and hauling represents a much greater concentration of Aboriginal employment as these activities account for only 28% of non-Aboriginal employment.

Table 3.7.   Distribution of ADM workforce[a] by employment area, 2003

		Assett management	Production mining	Production processing	Support areas	Total
Locally sourced	Aboriginal	23	43	6	13	85
	Non-Aboriginal	12	43	11	13	79
	Total	35	86	17	26	164
Fly-in/ Fly-out	Aboriginal	1	1	1	3	6
	Non-Aboriginal	124	125	65	100	414
	Total	125	126	66	103	420
Total	Aboriginal	24	44	7	16	91
	Non-Aboriginal	160	212	83	129	493
	Total	184	256	90	145	584

Note: a. Excluding contracted labour

Source: ADM Regional Business Development Unit

The future size and composition of the site-based workforce under the proposed underground mining phase is currently in design and subject to constant revision as uncertainties regarding work roles, shift lengths, and roster requirements are variously clarified. If the decision is made to proceed, the period between 2005 and 2012 will see substantial variation in workforce numbers with peaks and troughs evident before greater stability in workforce levels resumes with the focus solely on underground production and ore processing through to 2020. As Aboriginal employment targets are based on a proportional share of the total workforce, eventual numbers arising from these developments, if they occur, are equally uncertain at this point. However, as noted, the guiding principle is that at least half of the locally-sourced site-based workforce will be Aboriginal. On current indications (end of 2003), the size of the locally-sourced workforce by around 2013 will be in the region of 320 at 80% of the likely total workforce, and this will be a fairly steady figure throughout the rest of that decade. If half of these were Aboriginal this would translate into some 160 Aboriginal site-based workers. Compared to just 34 Aboriginal workers in 2001, this represents a substantial numeric increase. From a regional development perspective, the question is what impact would such an increase have on regional labour force status?

Estimating future labour force status

Clearly, the worsening economic status of Aboriginal people in the East Kimberley, as measured by the growing gap in relative regional incomes and increasing Aboriginal reliance on welfare, is to a large extent a function of their continued failure to adequately participate in the mainstream labour market. In recent years, the thrust of policy aimed at reducing welfare dependence and raising economic status has been towards increasing mainstream employment, especially in the private sector. As we have seen, this has not been adequately achieved, at least up to 2001. What then is the scale of the task ahead if the aims of policy remain the same, and what impact will the projected Argyle employment numbers have? To establish this, we can use the projection of the future size of the working age population shown in Table 2.7 and consider this against expected growth in employment.

Aboriginal population totals for the Northern East Kimberley projected to 2016 are shown in Table 3.8 by selected age groups, together with numeric and percentage change from the 2001 ERP. Overall, by 2016, the Indigenous population is projected to increase by 35% (or 2.3% per annum) to reach a population of 5,831—an increase of just over 1,500 persons. As shown by the percentage change by age group, much of this growth will occur in the working age groups with the adult population over 15 years increasing by more than 1,100. Realistically, a focussed age grouping would be more appropriate for establishing future needs, but even if those in the age range 15-44 are selected as the ones most likely to be targeted for emerging opportunities in the regional labour market in the years ahead, this age group is still set to increase by 763. What are the implications, then, of these projections for future Indigenous employment requirements?

The answer to this depends very much on future prospects for additional Aboriginal job creation. To estimate this, the observed rate of growth in Aboriginal employment in the East Kimberley as a whole between 1996 and 2001 (1.8% per annum) is continued for the projection period. However, included in this is an assumption that CDEP will account for all of the net growth in Aboriginal jobs over the projection period. This reflects the situation between 1996 and 2001 as Aboriginal numbers employed in mainstream work actually fell during this time by 30%. At the same time, CDEP growth is augmented by the anticipated new jobs for Aboriginal workers to be created at Argyle assuming that planned targets are achieved. As noted above, compared to 2001, this represents an additional 126 positions by 2016. Options for increased employment off-site via sub-contracting and joint venturing have not been included in this estimation for want of adequate data.

Table 3.8.   Aboriginal population of the Northern East Kimberley by selected age groups: 2001 and 2016

Age group	ERP 2001	Projection 2016	Net change	% change
0-4	606	784	178	29.3
5-14	1,069	1,353	284	26.6
15-24	843	1,146	303	35.9
25-44	1,145	1,605	460	40.2
45-64	483	783	294	60.1
65+	171	160	-11	-6.4
Total	4,317	5,831	1,514	35.1

Three future employment scenarios are explored in Table 3.9. The first considers the number of jobs that would be required by 2016 if the 2001 Indigenous employment/population ratio were to remain unchanged at 45.7% (inclusive of CDEP). The answer is 1,688 or an additional 481. With 490 additional jobs expected to be produced (364 from continued expansion of CDEP and 126 from ADM targets for local employment), this means that there will be just enough extra jobs to maintain the status quo in terms of the overall employment/population ratio. In effect, then, no impact on the current employment rate is envisaged.

The second scenario considers the extra jobs required to maintain the reported mainstream employment population ratio of 16.2%. This reveals that job growth net of CDEP will be insufficient to match growth in the working age population resulting in a deficit of 44 jobs and producing a reduction in the mainstream employment/population ratio from 16.2 to 15.0. The final scenario considers the future job requirements necessary to raise the Indigenous employment/population ratio to the mainstream level recorded for non-Aboriginal residents (81.3%). This produces a massive job deficit of 1,306 by 2016. In other words, the number of Aboriginal people in work across the Northern East Kimberley would need to more than double over the 15 year period with almost 100 extra jobs required each year—a task of an order of magnitude way beyond the capacity of current policy settings, and clearly in excess of any impact due to ADM targets despite the fact that these are ambitious.

Table 3.9.   Extra Aboriginal jobs required in the Northern East Kimberley by 2016

Employment/ population ratio in 2001	Base employment 2001	Total jobs required by 2016	Extra jobs required by 2016	Extra jobs likely by 2016	Jobs deficit by 2016
45.7[a]	1,207	1,688[d]	481	490[e]	9
16.2[b]	428	598	170	126	-44
81.3[c]	1,207	3,003	1,796	490[e]	-1,306

Notes: a. The 2001 census-derived Aboriginal employment/population ratio inclusive of CDEP

b. The 2001 census-derived Aboriginal employment/population ratio exclusive of CDEP (mainstream employment)

c. The non-Aboriginal census-derived employment/population ratio in 2001

d. Based on projection of working age population to 2016 (3,694)

e. Based on 1996-2001 Aboriginal regional employment growth rate of 1.8% p.a augmented by an additional 126 ADM jobs based on local employment targets

To summarise, because of the relative balance between projected population growth and anticipated employment growth, even if the substantial ADM employment targets for local Aboriginal people are met this will not result in any noticeable change in the Aboriginal employment/population ratio according to the assumptions applied because of the relatively small numbers involved. This estimation is inclusive of further growth in CDEP scheme employment. If the focus is solely on sustaining current mainstream employment rates, then the ADM targets are definitely insufficient to impact on regional labour force status.[2] In terms of actually improving Aboriginal labour force status to anything approaching the norm for non-Aboriginal residents of the region, this task is way beyond any impact that could emanate from employment at the mine site.

This last observation raises the fact that no estimation has been made here regarding any enhanced labour market opportunity that might result for Aboriginal people as a consequence of work experience and/or training gained at ADM. Certainly, the number of individuals with work experience at the mine will undoubtedly exceed the number of those in such employment at any one time given the nature of turnover in the mine workforce, and the question arises as to whether work experience at Argyle leads on to work elsewhere within the region thereby raising overall Aboriginal employment levels. Other regional multipliers for Aboriginal employment may also emanate in the form of sub-contracting and joint venturing with future mine operations, but the possible scale of these remains unknown at this stage. Having said that, some of this already occurs via intermediate labour market programs that are available to communities in the region to engage workers (often CDEP workers) in commercial-type operations with work experience on ADM related projects such as road maintenance. It is estimated by ADM that such activities could involve around 150 individuals over the next 5 years. More importantly, ADM has also established an Indigenous Employment and Training Strategy (2003-2007) with the Commonwealth Department of Employment and Workplace Relations (DEWR) worth $15m ($5m from DEWR and $10m from ADM) to provide employment and training for an additional 150 Aboriginal people via the ADM operation (Argyle Diamonds 2003). Aside from contributing to the achievement of ADM's Aboriginal employment targets, the aim here is as much about providing accredited and transportable skills to enhance the capacity of local Aboriginal people to engage the regional labour market.

Whatever impact on Aboriginal labour force participation might arise from these efforts in coming years, the experience in recent years of an overall regional decline in Aboriginal mainstream employment, and the enormity of the task in hand required to turn this around, suggests that all areas of the regional labour market will need to be opened up as potential avenues for increased Aboriginal employment. This is particularly so among major regional employment sectors (tourism, agriculture, retailing, State government services) from which Aboriginal people are notably absent. If each of these were to achieve the same Aboriginal employment and training targets set by ADM for future years, and even if they matched those already achieved by ADM, only then would positive impact on regional labour force status be evident.

Notes

1. In a statistical sense, segregation refers to the degree of difference in the pattern of proportional distribution between two otherwise similar sets of data. A relative measure of such difference is provided by a wide range of segregation indices, and one commonly used in studies of labour force segregation, the index of dissimilarity, is used here. This is calculated by summing the absolute difference between the percentage of all people employed in different industry categories and dividing the answer by two. Thus, an index g 17.8 indicates that 17.8 per cent of male (or female) workers would have to change their industry of employment if the distributions were to be the same.

2. This is especially so as the definition of 'locally-sourced' used for future workforce estimates is geographically wider than the Northern East Kimberley region leading to potentially greater numbers in the numerator than might occur if the narrower geography (which defines the denominator) was applied.

4. Employment and welfare income

Aboriginal people in the East Kimberley have a number of potential sources of cash income. These range from wage labour in CDEP, or in other more mainstream forms of work, unemployment benefit and other benefit payments from Centrelink, compensation or other agreed payments to traditional land owners, and private income from the sale of art works, crafts and other products. Set against these, of course, are routine deductions from income at source, such as those for house rent and power charges.

Accurate data on income levels, and employment and non-employment sources of income, are notoriously difficult to obtain due to a variety of conceptual problems. For one thing, most measures of income refer to a period of time, such as annual or weekly income, whereas the flow of income to individuals and households within the region is often intermittent. Census data, for example, are collected for all sources of income in respect of a 'usual week' and then rounded up to annual income. What might constitute 'usual weekly' income in many Aboriginal households is difficult to determine. On the credit side, there is the likelihood of intermittent employment and windfall gains from sources such as gambling, cash loans, art work, and compensation payments. This sort of income combines with debits, for example due to loss of employment and cash transfers to others, to create a highly complex picture even over a short space of time, and one that census methods of data gathering are likely to misrepresent.

Even if adequate questions were asked regarding income, high levels of population mobility would make it difficult to establish a consistent set of income recipients over a period of time. This is further complicated by job mobility with individuals often employed on a casual or part-time basis and moving into and out of longer-term jobs. As for the circulation of cash between individuals and households, information on this is non-existent. Also lacking are data on expenditure, although a common pattern reported from elsewhere is one of cash feast and famine against a background of high costs for essentials such as food and transport (Beck 1985: 89; Rowse 1988; Taylor and Westbury 2000).

The most comprehensive public source of income data for the region based on a consistent methodology is available from the census. It should be noted, however, that census data report income in categories, with the highest category left open-ended. Consequently, actual incomes have to be derived. In estimating total and mean incomes, the mid-point for each income category is used on the assumption that individuals are evenly distributed around this mid-point. The open-ended highest category is problematic, but it is arbitrarily assumed that the average income received by individuals in this category was one-and-a-half times the lower limit of the category.

Also, the gross income reported in the census is intended to include family allowances, pensions, unemployment benefits, student allowances, maintenance, superannuation, wages, salary, dividends, rents received, interest received, business or farm income, and worker's compensation received. Whether all such sources are reported is unknown. One distinct advantage of census data, however, is that it provides a means by which an estimate of dependence on income from welfare can be derived. This is done by cross-tabulating data on income with labour force status as a basis for distinguishing employment income from non-employment income, the latter being considered a proxy measure of welfare dependence.

Employment and non-employment income

The relative contribution made to total income from employment as opposed to from other sources is an important factor in the regional economy. Approximate parity between net incomes derived from social security and those derived from employment (after tax) is likely, unless there is access to well-paying jobs. It is argued generally for Aboriginal people that the gap between welfare and earned income is sufficiently low as to discourage job seeking (Hunter and Daly 1998). As we have seen, though, in the East Kimberley the issue is just as much about creating sufficient employment in the first place.

Table 4.1 shows Aboriginal and non-Aboriginal annual average personal incomes by labour force status separately for the population resident in towns (Kununurra, Wyndham and Halls Creek) and communities in the Northern East Kimberley. The ratios of Aboriginal to non-Aboriginal incomes for each of these categories are shown in Table 4.2. Clearly, employment in the mainstream labour market returns higher personal income compared to CDEP, especially in communities where most mainstream positions are in skilled occupations. However, Aboriginal people in mainstream work still lag behind their non-Aboriginal counterparts with income levels between 20% and 30% lower. The contrast in income levels is most marked among those in CDEP reflecting the gap between Aboriginal workers and non-Aboriginal administrators. Also of note is the fact that Aboriginal non-employment (welfare) income in communities is substantially lower than non-Aboriginal equivalent income, and compared to Aboriginal people in towns. Reasons for this are not clear, but it is worth asking whether this might reflect underpayment of benefits to community residents. Overall, average Aboriginal incomes are almost 70% lower than non-Aboriginal incomes in communities, and 66% lower in towns.

Table 4.1. Aboriginal and non-Aboriginal annual average personal income ($) by labour force status: Towns and communities in the Northern East Kimberley, 2001

	CDEP	Mainstream	Unemployed	Not in labour force	Total
Communities ($)					
Aboriginal	12,081	35,628	10,507	9,657	12,858
Non-Aboriginal	30,280	44,406	N/A[a]	12,931	39,917
Total	13,202	43,478	10,540	10,506	26,805
Towns ($)					
Aboriginal	11,397	26,691	9,014	11,360	14,582
Non-Aboriginal	30,810	37,873	9,939	12,588	33,149
Total	12,890	36,354	9,362	11,753	26,396

Note: a. N/A = not applicable

Source: Customised census tables

Table 4.2. Ratios of Aboriginal to non-Aboriginal annual average personal income ($) by labour force status: Towns and communities in the Northern East Kimberley, 2001

CDEP	Mainstream	Unemployed	Not in labour force	Total
		Communities		
0.39	0.80	N/A[a]	0.74	0.32
		Towns		
0.37	0.70	0.91	0.90	0.44

Note: a. N/A = not applicable

Source: Customised census tables

Welfare income

The actual dollar contribution to regional income from employment and non-employment (welfare) sources in 2001 is shown in Table 4.3. In this instance, the region referred to is the whole of the East Kimberley incorporating the two Shires. This is because comparison is sought with the situation in 1981 and at this time data on the characteristics of usual residents were only available at LGA level.

Table 4.3. Gross annual personal income ($) for Aboriginal and non-Aboriginal adult residents of the East Kimberley, 2001

	Aboriginal	Non-Aboriginal	Total	Aboriginal % share of income
CDEP	14,273,480	N/A[a]	14,273,480	N/A[a]
Mainstream	10,274,160	107,714,880	117,989,040	8.6
Unemployment	979,160	461,240	1,440,400	67.4
Not in the labour force	13,734,760	6,109,480	19,844,240	69.2
Total	39,261,560	114,285,600	153,547,160	25.5
Welfare share (ex CDEP)	0.35	0.05		
Welfare share (inc CDEP)	0.74	0.06		

Note: a. N/A = not applicable

Source: Customised census tables

According to these calculations, the total gross annual personal income accruing to East Kimberley adult residents in 2001 amounted to $153.5 million. However, only one-quarter of this ($39 million) went to Aboriginal residents despite the fact that they accounted for almost half (47%) of the adult population. Of greater interest is the fact that only 8% of the total regional income generated by mainstream employment accrued to Aboriginal people. The implications of this are reflected in relative levels of welfare dependency with 35% of total Aboriginal income attributable to non-employment (welfare) sources compared to only 5% of non-Aboriginal income. If CDEP income is also counted as welfare income owing to its notional link to Newstart Allowance, then the level of Aboriginal welfare dependency rises to 74%.

It is interesting to compare these 2001 levels and ratios with those recorded in 1981 at the commencement of mining at Argyle. These are shown in Table 4.4. Overall, the Aboriginal share of total regional income has risen from 20% to 25%. However, this masks some worrying trends in terms of income sources. Before considering these, it should be noted that due to the absence of CDEP in 1981, employment income recorded for that year is essentially derived from mainstream work. With this in mind, if the ratio of Aboriginal to non-Aboriginal mainstream employment income in 1981 is compared to that for 2001 (0.15 compared to 0.10), then it would appear that an income gap has opened up between Aboriginal and non-Aboriginal mainstream workers over the past 20 years. Accordingly, the Aboriginal share of total income from mainstream employment has fallen from 13% in 1981 to only 9% in 2001.

Table 4.4. **Gross annual personal income ($) for Aboriginal and non-Aboriginal adult residents of the East Kimberley, 1981**

	Aboriginal	Non-Aboriginal	Total	Aboriginal % share of income
Mainstream	3,764,500	25,481,000	29,245,500	12.7
Unemployment	282,000	168,500	450,500	62.6
Not in the labour force	2,459,000	775,500	3,234,500	75.0
Total	6,505,500	26,425,000	32,930,500	19.7
Welfare share	0.42	0.04		

Source: Customised census tables

At the same time, the level of Aboriginal welfare dependency appears to have dropped, although, as always, there is the vexed question of where to place CDEP income in such a calculation. If CDEP is counted as welfare income in 2001, then Aboriginal dependency for income from welfare sources can be seen to have risen from 42% in 1981 to 74% in 2001. If this finding holds, then it is exactly the opposite trajectory to that observed for non-Aboriginal residents of the region, whose dependency on welfare income is very low anyway. In short, using income as a key indicator of economic status, development of the regional economy over the 20 years since mining commenced at Argyle has raised the relative economic status of non-Aboriginal residents and reduced that of Aboriginal residents. Of the estimated gross Aboriginal income of $39.2 million for the East Kimberley as a whole in 2001, $27 million (69%) of this was due to residents of the study region.

However, non-Aboriginal residents of the same region were in receipt of fully $101 million (88%) of the $114 million attributed to the East Kimberley. This means that only 21% of total income in the study region accrued to Aboriginal residents, compared to 35% for the East Kimberley as a whole.

While it is not easy to directly compare estimates made from census data with those made from administrative records, in order to gain a clearer picture of the composition of welfare income, information was obtained from Centrelink regional office in Kununurra on the amounts paid in benefits (excluding CDEP) at each community in the study region for a single fortnight as close to the census date as possible (Table 4.5). It should be noted that these data are for the total population owing to difficulties with Indigenous identification in Centrelink records. It should also be noted that the annualised estimates shown are derived by simply multiplying the fortnightly payments by 26. This assumes, then, that the fortnightly payments indicated are constant throughout the year, which is unlikely to be the case.

Table 4.5.   Number and amount of Centrelink benefit payments made at each community in the Northern East Kimberley, 2001[a]

	Number of customers	Total amount of fortnightly benefits paid[a] ($)	Estimated annualised amount paid ($)
Kununurra	1,356	407,845	10,603,970
Wyndham	441	135,048	3,511,248
Halls Creek	1,166	354,400	9,214,400
Warmun	217	63,992	1,663,792
Mandangala	20	6,106	158,756
Woolah	17	2,849	74,074
Oombulgurri	91	28,863	750,438
Kalumburu	214	65,310	1,698,060
Total region	3,522	1,064,413	27,674,738

Note: a. As at 28 September

Source: Centrelink, Kununurra

From Table 4.3, it can be seen that in the East Kimberley as a whole, census-based estimates of annual welfare income (net of CDEP) accruing to the population amounted to around $21m. The interesting feature of Table 4.5, then, is that the Northern East Kimberley communities alone receive far more than this (an estimated $27m) each year. Of course, both estimates are likely to suffer methodological uncertainty. All that can be confidently stated is that the amount of annual welfare income paid out in the study region is over $20m, and that Aboriginal adults receive approximately 70% of this.

5. Education and training: participation and outcomes

There are two broad perspectives against which the purpose and performance of education in the region may be assessed. The first is culturally grounded and considers what Aboriginal people want from education. According to one analyst, with reference to Arnhem Land communities, many Aboriginal people selectively procure aspects of Western education and ignore others that do not suit their needs and aspirations (Schwab 1998). Consequently, what is desired from education in general, and from schools in particular, can be very different to what these Western institutions expect. These desires have been conceptualised in terms of the acquisition of core competencies to deal with the non-Aboriginal world, the capacity for cultural maintenance, and access to material and social resources (Schwab 1998: 15).

The second derives from an economic development model and stresses a need to acquire human capital skills in order to participate in the mainstream economy. From this perspective, educational outcomes are measured in terms of participation rates, grade progression, competency in numeracy and literacy skills, and, for the Vocational Education and Training sector, course completion. Given the need to develop a statistical profile of the regional population, and to draw comparison with non-Aboriginal people and Indigenous people elsewhere in the state, the entire focus here is on the second perspective. This is not to deny, though, that skills acquired outside formal educational processes cannot, and may not, lead to Aboriginal participation in the regional economy in other more informal ways. The problem for socio-economic profi ling is that these more culturally grounded attributes are more difficult to quantify and lack readily accessible data sources.

Participation in schooling

A total of 11 schools are located in the Northern East Kimberley. Three of these are administered by the Western Australian Catholic Education Office: Ngalangangpum (Warmun), St Joseph's (Kununurra), and St Joseph's (Wyndham). All of the others, with the exception of Purnululu school at Wurreranginy, are administered by the WA Department of Education: Halls Creek District High School, Kununurra District High School, Wyndham District High School, Dawul Remote Community School (Woolah), Jungdranung Remote Community School (Mandangala), Oombulgurri Remote Community School, and Kalumburu Remote Community School. While there are only 3 high schools in this list, all the state-run remote community schools, as well as Ngalangangpum School at Warmun, offer secondary years subject to demand. The St Joseph's schools in Wyndham and Kununurra are primary schools only with classes to year 7. In addition, the Barramundi school (now attached to Kununurra DHS) is designed on cultural lines and incorporates Indigenous people as staff, managers and advisers. This was established in 1995 to accommodate the educational needs of many Indigenous teenagers who had dropped out of conventional schooling. According to Sidoti (2000), Barramundi School aims to:

- create a discussion with the community about the needs of teenagers in terms of learning, employment, cultural maintenance and identity;

- bring 'schooling' to the community rather than the community to the school;

- involve traditional learning by community members as a basis for all learning that is done in the program.

Enrolments

In the first semester of 2001, a total of 1,657 enrolments were recorded in these schools between school years 1 and 10, which approximates the compulsory school age range of 5-17 years. According to school records, Aboriginal students accounted for the majority of these enrolments (1,085 or 65%). In addition, a total of 28 Aboriginal youth were enrolled in Year 11 and 12 classes, along with 35 non-Aboriginal youth. For a more precise estimate of school participation among the compulsory age population, data on the ages of students were obtained. These show that a total of 832 Aboriginal students of primary age (5-12 years) were enrolled in the second semester of 2001, representing 87% of the estimated resident Aboriginal population of the Northern East Kimberley in that age group. As for secondary ages (13-17 years), a total of 220 Aboriginal students were enrolled, representing 46% of the eligible population. Overall, the Aboriginal enrolment rate among the regional population of compulsory school age was 73%. While some uncertainty surrounds this figure owing to an unknown degree of concordance between the numerator enrolment data and denominator population data, it nonetheless suggests that a substantial proportion of Aboriginal children of school age within the Northern East Kimberley do not enrol at school, especially at secondary level. These participation rates are lower than equivalent state-level figures. In 1996, the rate of Indigenous participation at primary level for the whole of Western Australia was 93%, and 62% for secondary level (Government of Western Australia 2003: 103).

Actual enrolment numbers in each school in the Northern East Kimberley are presented in Table 5.1 (enrolments in the Barramundi school in 2001 were small—10 boys and 10 girls). Clearly, with the exception of Kununurra District High School, all schools in the study region have a majority Aboriginal enrolment. Indeed, given the dynamics of the regional population over the past 20 years, it is possible to suggest a trend towards the Aboriginalisation of the region's school population. An extreme example is provided by Wyndham High School. In 1982, this school had a total of 278 enrolments, 34% of which were Aboriginal. By 2001, total enrolments were down to 132, and 80% of these were Aboriginal.

Table 5.1. Aboriginal and non-Aboriginal enrolments[a] at schools in the Northern East Kimberley, 2001

School	Aboriginal enrolments	Non-Aboriginal enrolments	Aboriginal % of Total enrolments
Halls Creek DHS	227	13	94.6
Wyndham DHS	105	27	79.5
Kununurra DHS	228	441	34.1
Dawul RCS	18	0	100.0
Jungdranung RCS	22	0	100.0
Oombulgurri RCS	55	0	100.0
Kalumburu RCS	111	0	100.0
St Joseph's Wyndham	59	8	88.1
St Joseph's Kununurra	136	83	62.1
Ngalanganpum	94	0	100.0
Purnululu	30	0	100.0
Total	1,085	572	65.5

Note: a. Figures refer to enrolments in years 1-12

Source: WA Department of Education

Retention rates

Table 5.2 shows apparent retention rates for Aboriginal students in government schools in the Northern East Kimberley from year 8 to year 10, and from year 10 to year 12. These rates are compared with those recorded for Indigenous students generally in Western Australia, as well as with all students in the State. For each year between 1998 and 2001 the rates represent the proportion of those previously in year 8 who were retained by year 10, with the same calculation made in respect of those previously in year 10 retained by year 12. Taking the state-wide situation first, this reveals that for all students in Western Australia, retention rates from year 8 to year 10 are high and generally close to 100%. However, the retention of Indigenous students across the state to year 10 is notably lower at around 85%. In Northern East Kimberley schools, the equivalent rates vary from year to year, but are generally lower again averaging 82% in remote community schools, and 76% in the district high schools.

Table 5.2.   **Apparent retention rates for Aboriginal and all students in Western Australian and Northern East Kimberley government schools: 1998–2001**

Apparent retention rates	1998	1999	2000	2001
Year 8 to year 10				
WA Total	98.2	98.3	99.0	100.0
WA Indigenous	N/A[c]	85.5	84.1	84.9
Study region RCS[a] Aboriginal students	84.2	80.0	77.2	87.5
Study region DHS[b] Aboriginal students	74.6	88.0	67.8	75.0
Year 10 to year 12				
WA Total	67.6	67.8	67.3	67.0
WA Indigenous	N/A[c]	23.6	26.9	21.0
Study region RCS Aboriginal students	0.0	17.6	18.7	0.0
Study region DHS Aboriginal students	15.1	22.2	12.0	20.4

Notes: a. RCS = Remote Community Schools

b. DHS = District High Schools

c. N/A = Not applicable

Source: WA Department of Education; Commonwealth of Australia 2003: Table 3A:72

From a labour market perspective, retention to year 12 from year 10 is of greater significance (ABS/CAEPR 1996). For all students in Western Australia, this rate falls to a consistent level of 67%, and statewide Indigenous rates fall much further, ranging between 21% and 27%. In the Northern East Kimberley, the rate of retention of Aboriginal students to Year 12 is even lower again, averaging only 17% since 1998. As a consequence, in each of the years between 1998 and 2001 an average of only 9 Aboriginal students has been enrolled in year 12 in Northern East Kimberley government schools compared to an average of 58 in year 10.

The impact of these retention rates is reflected in census data on the highest levels of schooling completed as reported by adults (those over 15 years) in each community. These levels are shown in Table 5.3 for Aboriginal adults in each of the IAs in the study region, while equivalent figures for non-Aboriginal adults as a whole are also provided for comparative purposes. For the most part, the proportion of Aboriginal adults completing school at particular levels is broadly similar throughout the region, although Oombulgurri reports an above average proportion completing year 10, and Kalumburu an above average share of those completing only year 8 or below. At the same time, Warmun, Halls Creek, Halls Creek (n), and Wyndham-East Kimberley (w) report relatively high proportions of adults who have never been to school, no doubt reflecting the preponderance of older people in these areas whose formative years were spent on cattle properties mostly away from mission and government influence. In Warmun, for example, 22% of adult census respondents reported that they had never attended school. As for the overall situation, the main contrast within the study region between the Aboriginal and non-Aboriginal population is the fact that almost 40% of Aboriginal adults left school before year 10, while the same percentage of non-Aboriginal adults completed year 12. As numerous studies based on census and survey data have shown (ABS/CAEPR 1996; Daly 1995; Gray, Hunter and Schwab 2000; Hunter 2002; Hunter and Schwab 2003), this contrast in levels of schooling completed is highly significant in terms of explaining differential rates of Aboriginal and non-Aboriginal participation in mainstream employment.

Table 5.3. **Highest level of schooling completed: Aboriginal and non-Aboriginal adults in the Northern East Kimberley, 2001**

Indigenous Area	Year 8 or below	Year 9	Year 10	Year 11	Year 12	Still at school	Did not go to school
	Aboriginal adults						
Kununurra	21.4	12.8	28.6	14.0	10.8	3.7	8.6
Wyndham	23.3	11.7	28.3	10.0	6.3	2.3	3.7
Halls Creek	22.0	14.4	25.8	7.9	10.3	2.0	14.2
Kalumburu	47.6	26.2	7.9	3.7	4.9	4.9	4.9
Oombulgurri	9.9	10.9	68.3	7.9	3.0	0.0	0.0
Lake Argyle	21.0	18.9	30.1	11.2	11.2	2.1	5.6
Wyndham-E. Kim (w)	22.4	12.8	31.2	12.0	0.0	0.0	14.4
Warmun	9.2	15.6	31.2	8.7	9.8	3.5	22.0
Halls Creek (n)	30.4	8.8	32.8	4.8	4.8	2.4	16.0
Total (Aboriginal)	23.5	14.8	29.5	9.6	8.4	2.6	10.7
Total (non-Aboriginal)	6.8	8.0	30.4	12.6	39.0	0.6	0.2

Note: Rows add up to 100%

Source: ABS 2001 Census of Population and Housing

Attendance

For most schools in the Northern East Kimberley, the educational impact of relatively low levels of Aboriginal school enrolment is compounded by low Aboriginal school attendance, although Aboriginal attendance rates at many of the region's schools are actually higher than the equivalent State average. Table 5.4 shows Aboriginal and non-Aboriginal attendance averages for enrolments at government schools in the study region in 2001. Aboriginal State averages for remote community schools and district high schools are also provided for comparative purposes.

Table 5.4.   **Aboriginal and non-Aboriginal attendance rates in Northern East Kimberley government schools, 2001**

	Aboriginal	Non-Aboriginal	Aboriginal State averages
Jungdranung RCS[a]	78.7	N/A[c]	77.5 (RCS)
Dawul RCS	94.4	N/A[c]	77.5 (RCS)
Oombulgurri RCS	93.3	N/A[c]	77.5 (RCS)
Kalumburu RCS	86.9	N/A[c]	77.5 (RCS)
Wyndham DHS[b]	84.0	91.7	79.5 (DHS)
Kununurra DHS	81.3	93.7	79.5 (DHS)
Halls Creek DHS	55.9	93.7	79.5 (DHS)

Notes   a. RCS = Remote Community Schools

b. DHS = District High Schools

c. N/A = Not applicable

Source: WA Department of Education

With the exception of Halls Creek High School, attendance rates for Aboriginal students in the region compare favourably with the State average, especially at Oombulgurri and Dawul schools where they are on a par with the rates recorded for local non-Aboriginal students. By contrast, attendance rates at Halls Creek High School fall substantially below all other benchmarks. Comparison of Figure 5.1 for Halls Creek High School with Figures 5.2 and 5.3 for Wyndham High School and Kununurra High School respectively, shows that this relative lack of attendance occurs at all ages, but especially in the primary years 5 and 6.

Figure 5.1.   **Aboriginal and non-Aboriginal attendance rates by school year: Halls Creek District High School, 2001**

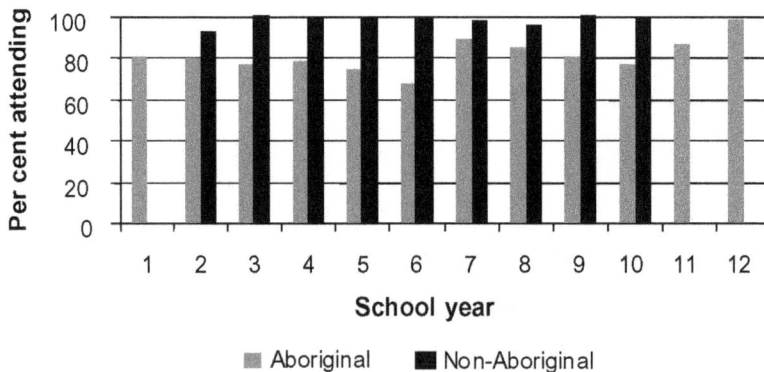

Figure 5.2.   Aboriginal and non-Aboriginal attendance rates by school year: Wyndham
              District High School, 2001

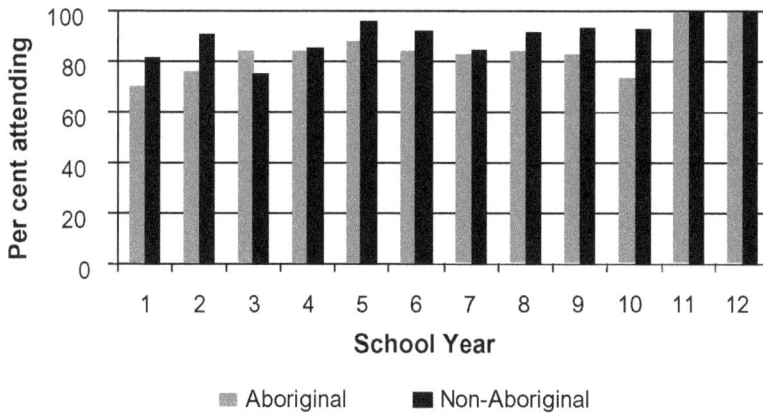

Figure 5.3.   Aboriginal and non-Aboriginal attendance rates by school year: Kununurra
              District High School, 2001

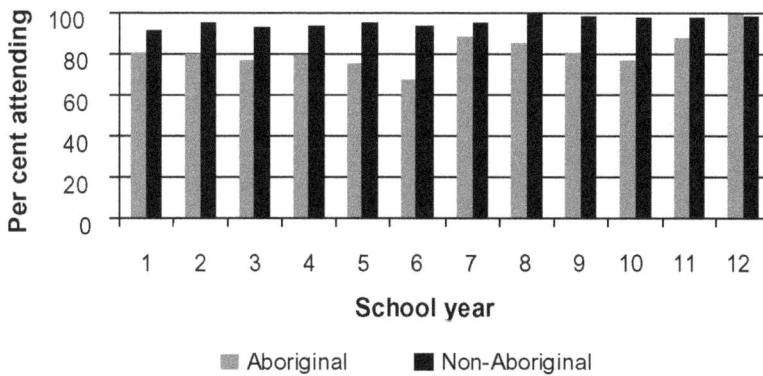

All these official data and estimates regarding school access and participation are based on averages. What they do not show, and what would be more important to reveal (if it were possible), are the day-to-day levels of individual attendance at school. Given the variability in attendance and high level of population mobility, it cannot be assumed that aggregate data refer consistently to the same individuals. Since children often accompany adults in their movements across, into and out of the region it seems likely that some mobile children may be overlooked as part of the regular school population. Moreover, because attendance registers are taken each morning, no records exist regarding student participation beyond morning sessions. The prospect thus exists that the attendance rates presented here, especially those for Aboriginal students, are overly favourable. Certainly, more detailed attendance data by individual school terms available from Ngalangangpum school at Warmun point to high variability in attendance throughout the year with as few as 30% of students in attendance in some school terms, compared to 80% in others. On average, though, these data indicate attendance rates in primary years ranging between 40% and 60%, with a discernable pattern of declining attendance from the beginning of the school year to the end, although why this should be so remains unclear.

Outcomes

As already noted, from the standpoint of participation in regional economic development, educational achievement is a key prerequisite. While studies reveal a clear positive relationship between economic status and level of educational achievement (ABS/CAEPR 1996), an important shortcoming is their lack of measurement of the quality of education outcomes. For example, age at leaving school or highest level of schooling completed does not necessarily equate with school-leaving grade level achievement. In fact, for many Aboriginal students in remote areas, age or grade level is a poor indicator of achievement as many Aboriginal students perform substantially below their age and grade levels in terms of literacy and numeracy competencies. Thus, while data on participation in the education system provide an important indication of access and utilisation, it should be noted that they are less revealing about outcomes in terms of demonstrated ability, no matter from what perspective this might be measured.

In Western Australia, outcomes from education are measured using benchmarks devised by the Western Australian Literacy and Numeracy Assessment program (WALNA). This is a curriculum-based assessment that tests students' knowledge and skills in numeracy, reading, spelling and writing. The WALNA test is administered annually to all students in Western Australian schools (including Catholic schools) in years 3, 5 and 7, although a few exemptions are made. The test gathers information on the performance of school children in relation to nationally agreed benchmarks in numeracy, reading, spelling and writing, and in relation to that of other Year 3, 5 or 7 students across Western Australia. The national benchmark standard is an agreed standard of performance that professional educators across the country deem to be the minimum level required for students at particular key stages in their educational development in order to make adequate progress. By providing an indication of how students are faring against the national benchmark and in relation to state performance, the WALNA assessment assists in identifying those students who would benefit from extension, as well as those not meeting the minimum expected standard.

For students in the Northern East Kimberley who sat the WALNA test (most of those eligible) in each of the core competencies, the percentage who achieved the benchmark cut-off score in 2002 is shown in Table 5.5 with comparative data for the whole State. These figures include all schools, both government and Catholic. As might be expected, given the relative school attendance rates observed above, the performance of Aboriginal students in the study region is substantially below that of their non-Aboriginal counterparts. Typically, the proportion of Aboriginal students achieving the benchmark in each school year and for each of the competencies, is less than 50%. The main exception is in year 5 for numeracy, reading and writing where Aboriginal performance peaks and is closest to local non-Aboriginal outcomes. A similar conclusion is drawn if comparison is made between outcomes in the region and those observed generally for Aboriginal students in Western Australia, although in some instances (notably year 5 reading and writing), students in the region perform above the Aboriginal state average. The last panel in Table 5 underscores the fact that performance generally in the Northern East Kimberley falls considerably below the State average for all students.

Table 5.5. **Percentage of Aboriginal and non-Aboriginal students meeting the WALNA benchmark for numeracy, reading, writing and spelling in Northern East Kimberley and Western Australian schools, 2002**

	Numeracy	Reading	Writing	Spelling
Aboriginal students in the Northern East Kimberley				
Year 3	31.1	53.7	30.0	15.4
Year 5	52.4	76.4	59.5	28.0
Year 7	21.4	22.1	39.4	17.3
Non-Aboriginal students in the Northern East Kimberley				
Year 3	76.8	86.5	80.7	77.7
Year 5	92.3	92.3	88.5	53.1
Year 7	80.9	82.6	71.7	46.0
Aboriginal students in Western Australia				
Year 3	57.8	77.5	54.7	51.5
Year 5	48.8	73.0	56.9	47.0
Year 7	38.4	42.4	38.0	40.6
All students in Western Australia				
Year 3	86.7	94.4	85.6	84.8
Year 5	85.9	94.4	87.6	80.5
Year 7	81.0	84.9	77.7	76.8

Source: WA Department of Education customised tables, WALNA website

Outcomes at the Barramundi school are framed somewhat differently. For example, aside from permanent teaching staff and Aboriginal education workers, many community members also participate in the school, and this may be viewed as a positive outcome. Examples include the police who teach defensive driving, the Aboriginal Medical Service which teaches first aid, TAFE which teaches welding, and elders who teach law (Sidoti 2000). Community agencies also offer work experience placements for Barramundi students, including the Kimberley Land Council, the youth centre and the police station. Barramundi School was evaluated by Edith Cowan University in 1999 and was found to be successful in raising attendance rates to over 85%; raising student literacy and numeracy levels; reducing offending—(crime among the Barramundi boys dropped from 80% in

1998 to 20% in 1999 and the 20% was committed during school holidays); and through gaining strong community and student approval (Sidoti 2000).

Participation in vocational education and training (VET)

Post-secondary education and training leading to the acquisition of formal qualifications is available from a variety of public and private providers in the region, ranging from the Kimberley College of TAFE with campuses at Wyndham, Kununurra and Halls Creek, to Argyle mine and local CDEP schemes. Table 5.6 shows the number and proportion of Aboriginal and non-Aboriginal enrolments in TAFE courses in the East Kimberley by course level in 2001. Almost one quarter of all Aboriginal male enrolments (22%) and 15% of Aboriginal female enrolments are in short, miscellaneous enabling courses with no formal certification attached. This compares to only 9% and 8% respectively for non-Aboriginal enrolments. Of those Aboriginal students enrolled in certified courses, the majority are at certificate I and II level, especially among males, whilst non-Aboriginal enrolments are far more likely to be at certificate III level or above. One noticeable variation from this pattern is the much higher proportion of Aboriginal females enrolled in diploma courses, although this only amounts to 18 persons. Also noticeable, is the fact that no enrolments were recorded at advanced diploma level, with the exception of one Aboriginal male.

Table 5.6.   **Aboriginal and non-Aboriginal VET enrolments[a] by course level: East Kimberley, 2001**

Course level	Aboriginal				Non-Aboriginal			
	Males		Females		Males		Females	
	No.	%	No.	%	No.	%	No.	%
No level[b]	66	22.5	43	15.1	21	9.4	23	8.7
1	136	46.4	82	28.8	47	21.1	51	19.3
2	50	17.1	82	28.8	49	22.0	82	31.1
3	31	10.6	53	18.6	75	33.6	89	33.7
4	2	0.7	7	2.5	28	12.6	13	4.9
5	7	2.4	18	6.3	3	1.3	6	2.3
6	1	0.3	0	0.0	0	0.0	0	0.0
Total	293	100.0	285	100.0	223	100.0	264	100.0

Notes: a. Includes all VET enrolments collected by the WA Department of Training from publicly funded providers (TAFES and universities) and from private providers receiving public funds. Enrolment data for Private providers undertaking VET activity on a fee-for-service basis are not collected by the Department of Training
b. 1. Certificate I. 2. Certificate II. 3. Certificate III. 4. Certificate IV. 5. Diploma. 6. Advanced diploma
Excludes Indigenous status not stated

Source: WA Department of Training

Outcomes

To measure performance in the VET sector, the Western Australian Department of Training and Employment has identified a number of key performance measures relating to efficiency, effectiveness and quality. In relation to the effectiveness of the training system, the key indicator is the rate of successful completion of modules—the components from which courses are constructed. Table 5.7 compares the rates of successful module completion for Aboriginal and non-Aboriginal males and females enrolled in East Kimberley training courses in 2002. Clearly, outcomes for Aboriginal males are the least favourable compared to both non-Aboriginal males and to Aboriginal females. Barely half of the enrolled Aboriginal males successfully completed their module, with one fifth failing and almost one quarter withdrawing before completion. Aboriginal females performed much better in 2002, although their rate of withdrawal from training modules was twice that of their non-Aboriginal counterparts.

Table 5.7.   VET module outcomes for Aboriginal and non-Aboriginal students[a] in the East Kimberley, 2001

	Aboriginal		Non-Aboriginal	
	Males	Females	Males	Females
Successfully completed[b]	54.1	71.4	86.3	80.8
Failed	21.1	12.0	7.2	10.6
Withdrawn	24.8	16.6	6.4	8.6
Total no.	1,041	441	799	601
Total %	100.0	100.0	100.0	100.0

Notes: a. Excludes those enrolled in modules and who are continuing studies into the next collection period

b. Successfully completed modules include those assessed as 'passed', or 'no assessment satisfactory completion of class hours', and 'status (or credit) gained through recognition of prior learning'

Source: Western Australia Department of Training

The module load completion rate (MLCR) provides another measure of performance and with this indicator it is possible to compare data for the East Kimberley with data for all of Western Australia (Table 5.8). The MLCR represents the sum of student curriculum hours for successfully completed modules expressed as a proportion of the total student curriculum hours across all module enrolments. In 2002, this rate was only 52% for Aboriginal module enrolments in the East Kimberley—two thirds of the level reported for non-Aboriginal students both in the East Kimberley and in Western Australia as a whole.

Table 5.8.   Aboriginal and non-Aboriginal average module load completion rates: East Kimberley and Western Australia, 2001

East Kimberley Aboriginal	East Kimberley Non-Aboriginal	Western Australia total
52.4%	77.3%	72.7%

Source: Western Australia Department of Training

Table 5.9. **Field of study of post-secondary qualifications: Aboriginal and non-Aboriginal adults in the Northern East Kimberley, 2001**

	Aboriginal				Non-Aboriginal			
	Males	Females	Persons Total	Persons %	Males	Females	Persons Total	Persons %
Natural & Physical Sciences	0	0	0	0.0	45	24	69	2.7
Information Technology	0	0	0	0.0	11	10	21	0.8
Engineering & Related Technologies	31	3	34	20.4	741	26	767	30.0
Architecture & Building	12	0	12	7.2	172	5	177	6.9
Agriculture, Environmental & Related Studies	3	3	6	3.6	144	33	177	6.9
Health	9	22	31	18.6	57	237	294	11.5
Education	0	13	13	7.8	83	221	304	11.9
Management & Commerce	4	32	36	21.6	134	174	308	12.1
Society & Culture	3	14	17	10.2	79	131	210	8.2
Creative Arts	0	3	3	1.8	24	32	56	2.2
Food, Hospitality & Personal Services	6	3	9	5.4	61	83	144	5.6
Mixed Field Programs	0	0	0	0.0	0	3	3	0.1
Field of Study inadequately described	6	0	6	3.6	17	7	24	0.9
Not stated	111	111	222	N/A[a]	164	83	247	N/A[a]
Total (ex n/s)	74	93	167	100.0	1,568	986	2,554	100.0

Note: a. N/A = not applicable

Source: ABS 2001 Census of Population and Housing

Qualifications

At the end of the day, a key element of human capital in the regional labour market, and a primary product of the education and training system, is an individual's acquisition of formal qualifications. While program data can reveal numbers passing through courses, it remains the case that the five-yearly census provides the most comprehensive source of data on the number of individuals within the Northern East Kimberley who currently hold post-secondary qualifications.

At the 2001 Census, a total of 179 Aboriginal adults in the East Kimberley as a whole reported having some form of post-school qualification. This represented just 5% of all adults. Translating these data to estimates of the resident Aboriginal population in the Northern East Kimberley produces an estimate of 132 Aboriginal adults in the region who held some form of post-secondary qualification in 2001, and some 2,500 who did not. By comparison, 50% of non-Aboriginal adults enumerated in the East Kimberley reported having a post-secondary qualification. This relative lack of post-secondary certification among the adult Aboriginal population is typical of the situation found generally in Western Australia, although in 2001 the Wunan ATSIC region reported the second lowest rate of qualification of all ATSIC Regions in the state (5% compared to 4% in Warburton).

For those Aboriginal census respondents who indicated their level of qualification, only 2% reported a Graduate Diploma; 13% had a Bachelor degree; 11% had an Advanced Diploma; and 74% had a certificate. By contrast, almost one-third of qualified non-Aboriginal respondents (32%) indicated a Bachelor degree or higher, 18% reported an Advanced Diploma, and 50% held a Certificate. Differences are also evident in the field of qualification reported, both by sex and by Aboriginality (Table 5.9), although high non-response to the census question on field of qualification undermines the quality of the data. It appears that most qualifications held by Aboriginal males are in engineering and building, not unlike their non-Aboriginal counterparts. Among both Aboriginal and non-Aboriginal females, on the other hand, qualifications in health, education and management predominate. These differences in field of qualification are broadly in line with occupational variations observed in the region between males and females, regardless of Aboriginality.

6. Housing and infrastructure

By the beginning of the 1980s, the migration of Aboriginal people off East Kimberley pastoral properties and in to urban areas and emergent communities had placed considerable strain on available housing stock in the region and added to the pressures for new dwelling construction. At the 1981 Census, a total of 295 Aboriginal dwellings were identified in the Northern East Kimberley, housing a total of 1,835 residents to produce an average occupancy rate of 6.2 persons per dwelling. However, 17% of these dwellings were improvised shelters or caravans, and so the average occupancy rate calculated as a ratio of standard housing at that time was 7.5 persons per dwelling. These rates are calculated using the actual census counts of residents in Aboriginal dwellings as the base. However, as observed in Chapter 2, the derived Indigenous ERP for the East Kimberley in 1981 was 13% higher than the census count. Thus, more realistic occupancy rates based on a higher regional population estimate (2,073) would have been 7.0 for all dwellings and 8.5 persons per standard dwelling.

Of course, these are average figures and the situation in many localities at that time reflected much higher overcrowding—12.5 persons per dwelling at Mirima, for example (Waringarri Aboriginal Association 1985: 14). While a backlog of community-managed housing stock was evident, so too was a backlog in the supply of State housing. In 1985, in Kununurra alone, a total of 130 extra houses were considered necessary simply to reduce Aboriginal occupancy levels to 6.5 persons per dwelling. At that time, there were only 38 'Aboriginal Grant Houses' available in town, while 20 Aboriginal families were accommodated in standard public housing, leading to an estimated shortfall of 72 dwellings (Waringarri Aboriginal Association 1985: 14).

In the ensuing two decades, difficulties in overcoming the backlog in housing needs have been compounded by rapid population growth and increased population dispersion across some 55 discrete communities and outstations within the Northern East Kimberley, 80% of which have less than 50 residents. Not surprisingly, in 1991, a normative measure of housing need found that the Wunan ATSIC Regional Council area had the fifth highest level of family 'homelessness' and overall housing need (defined for statistical purposes as families in improvised homes, or sharing overcrowded dwellings) out of the 36 ATSIC regions nationwide (Jones 1994: 61-4).

In the following year (1992), the first CHINS identified 439 dwellings owned or administered by Aboriginal organisations in the Wunan ATSIC Region (Australian Construction Services 1992). Of these, as many as 41% were found to be improvised shelters which suggests that either the 1981 Census grossly undercounted such dwellings, or that their number greatly increased over the decade due to a lack of standard housing supply. While the remaining dwellings identified in the 1992 CHINS were separate houses, 58% of these were found to be in need of some repair with more than one-third requiring major repairs or replacement. The total cost of meeting the identified Aboriginal housing needs of the region was estimated at $56.5 million, a figure that represented almost one-third of the total estimate for the whole of Western Australia. As for infrastructure, 33% of discrete communities in the

Wunan ATSIC Region had water quality below NHMRC guidelines, 23% had no water supply system, 25% had no sewage disposal system, 77% had no health buildings within the community, 38% had no electricity supply, 55% had no educational facilities, and 85% had no community store (Australian Construction Services 1992). In all of this, a degree of correlation between settlement size and remote location was observed.

The major response to such inadequacies was led by the Commonwealth and developed out of the National Aboriginal Health Strategy (NAHS) in 1990. This recognised an essential link between health outcomes and the provision of housing and infrastructure to acceptable minimum standards. Accordingly, funding allocations in the initial years of the NAHS primary health and environmental health programs included amounts directed at housing and infrastructure services within ATSIC's Community Housing and Infrastructure Program (CHIP). However, a review of CHIP in 1994 identified a range of problems, including a failure to address housing and infrastructure needs in a holistic way. Because of the short-term nature of the program-based approach to funding, communities were being required to structure housing needs to the CHIP program rather than the other way around (ATSIC 1994). A key response to these criticisms was the establishment in 1994 of the Health Infrastructure Priority Projects (HIPP) program to pilot new delivery arrangements for the construction of Aboriginal community housing and infrastructure.

In Western Australia, elements of NAHS/HIPP were incorporated into a 1997 bilateral agreement between the State government and ATSIC for the provision of housing and related infrastructure to Aboriginal people in the State. This arrangement has recently been updated after review in 2000 with an agreement to pool funding from the Commonwealth, ATSIC and the Western Australian government for the provision of Aboriginal housing and infrastructure under the auspices of an Aboriginal Housing and Infrastructure Council. In 2002/03 the Wunan ATSIC Regional Council allocated $6.3 million to this process and this represented 24% of the total ATSIC allocation for CHIP and the Remote Area Essential Services Program across the State (sourced from: *An Agreement for the provision of Housing and Infrastructure for Aboriginal and Torres Strait Islander People in Western Australia July 2002–June 2007*). If this same proportion of all other funds pooled under the agreement were also to be allocated to the Wunan ATSIC Region this would add a further $8 million. While these indicative dollars provide a measure of current inputs aimed at resolving the regional housing crisis, it is data from the 1997 WA Environmental Health Survey, the 2001 Census, and the 2001 CHINS that provide the essential baseline profile of housing and infrastructure outputs, as well as a means of assessing the net cumulative impact of such measures to date.

Housing and infrastructure in 2001

The five-yearly census is an enumeration of population and *housing*. It provides a range of details regarding the number and structure of dwellings and it is possible to classify these according to Aboriginal or non-Aboriginal occupancy and other housing-related variables.

Table 6.1 shows the number and type of Aboriginal and non-Aboriginal dwellings in the Northern East Kimberley with the former classified as such if one or more adults in a dwelling are Aboriginal.

Table 6.1. Structure of dwellings and occupancy rates: Northern East Kimberley, 2001

	Aboriginal dwellings			Non-Aboriginal dwellings		
	Dwellings	Persons	Occupancy rate	Dwellings	Persons	Occupancy rate
Separate house	561	2,990	5.4	899	2,399	2.7
Town house/ apartment	53	150	2.9	177	247	1.4
Improvised and other dwellings	94	365	3.9	231	345	1.5
Total[a]	717	3,574	5.0	1,348	3,019	2.2

Note: a. Includes structure of dwelling not stated

Source: ABS 2002

In 2001, a total of 2,065 dwelling units were recorded in the Northern East Kimberley.[1] Of these 717 (35%) were Aboriginal dwellings, most of which were separate houses, although 13% were improvised dwellings and caravans. Thus, the proportion of improvised Aboriginal dwellings had fallen only slightly (from 17%) since 1981. While most non-Aboriginal dwellings were also separate houses, the key point of distinction is the much higher average occupancy rate in Aboriginal dwellings—more than twice that recorded for non-Aboriginal dwellings (5.0 compared to 2.3), although it should be noted that, away from the towns of Kununurra, Wyndham and Halls Creek, the average Aboriginal occupancy rate increases to 7.0. As a benchmark, it is interesting to compare this rate with the average of 3.7 persons per Aboriginal dwelling recorded for Western Australia as a whole in 2001. Once again, however, these rates are based on actual census counts. Using the 2001 ERP as the base produces a revised overall Aboriginal occupancy rate of 5.7, and a figure of 8.0 for non-urban communities.

Thus, in the 20 years since mining commenced at Argyle, the overall regional occupancy rate for Aboriginal dwellings has been reduced, but only slightly from 7.0 to 5.7 persons per dwelling, and it remains substantially above the State average. Aboriginal people in the region are also now marginally more likely to be accommodated in conventional housing, but the indication is that provision of such housing has only just kept ahead of increased demand due to new household formation, with only limited impact on the aggregate level of overcrowding.

While continuing high Aboriginal occupancy rates partly reflect larger Aboriginal household size and a cultural preference for extended family living arrangements, it is also a measure of the inadequacy of housing stock available to accommodate the regional population. To acquire a better sense of the adequacy of housing, occupancy rates must be set against dwelling size and one measure of this is provided by the ratio of available bedrooms to the population in dwellings. Overall, in the Northern East Kimberley, the census recorded a total of 5,208 bedrooms in 2001. Of these, 1,836 (35%) were in Aboriginal dwellings (645 in communities and 1,191 in towns). Using the number of persons per dwelling inflated to match the ERP, this produces an average figure of 2.2 persons per bedroom in Aboriginal dwellings, with no difference apparent between town and country. The equivalent figure for non-Aboriginal dwellings is less than 1.0.

More refined measures also include an indication of housing affordability as well as functionality from an environmental health perspective. Applying basic overcrowding measures, Jones (1994) identified the Wunan ATSIC Region as ranked 5th highest out of 36 ATSIC Regions across the country in 1991 in terms of the size of its unmet housing need calculated on the basis of additional bedrooms required to meet an accepted occupancy rate. At that time, almost 60% of families were found to be in overcrowded dwellings (Jones 1994: 54) and the total extra bedroom need to overcome this was estimated at around 1,000. By 1996, the number of overcrowded households in the Wunan Regional Council area was still high at 45% and the region ranked 8th highest in the country (Jones 1999: 24), with a total extra bedroom need of 756 (Jones 1999: 38). In both years, the East Kimberley region stood out as having the greatest Aboriginal housing need of all Western Australian regions. While similar calculations have not been made using 2001 Census data owing to their complexity, the simple fact that the overall Aboriginal occupancy rate in 2001 is only slightly lower than recorded in 1981 suggests that overcrowding levels remain little altered.

This is supported by data from the 2001 CHINS, and a Wunan ATSIC Regional Council survey of community housing conducted in March 2003. The combined findings from these sources are presented in Table 6.2 which shows the number of dwellings, the estimated maximum population, and derived occupancy rates for each community and outstation in the Northern East Kimberley. The overall occupancy rate was 7.1 persons per Aboriginal dwelling, which is very close to that recorded by the 2001 Census for non-urban communities in the study region. It also accords exactly with the findings of a housing survey conducted in Warmun community in March 1998. However, this masks considerable diversity of circumstance, with occupancy rates ranging from 28 persons per dwelling in some instances to just one in others. Of particular note, however, is the fact that the larger communities of Warmun and Kalumburu have occupancy rates above the regional average, as do a number of town-based communities such as Mirima in Kununurra, and Mardiwa Loop in Halls Creek.

Table 6.2. Number of dwellings and occupancy rates in Aboriginal communities and outstations in the Northern East Kimberley, 2003

Locality	Max Pop Wet/Dry Season	Total No. of dwellings	Average No. people per dwelling
Alligator Hole	12	1	12
Bell Springs	20	2	10
Bow River	30	10	3
Cockatoo Springs	20	4	5
Crocodile Hole	15	7	2.1
Darlu Darlu (Nine Mile)	7	2	3.5
Dillon Springs	6	2 Sheds	3
Dingo Springs (Yardangarli)	6	1	6
Dolly Hole	10	2	5
8 Mile Bore (Galburring)	0	1	0
Emu Creek	30	4	7.5
Flying Fox Hole	0	2	0
Flywell	8	1	8
4 Mile	10	2	5
Frog Hollow	50	8	6.25
Gebowama	1	1 Shed	1
Glen Hill (Mandangala)	60	13	4.6
Goose Hill	6	0	6
Guda Guda	30	7	4.3
Honeymoon Beach	12	1	12
Kalumburu	500	38	13.1
Koongie Park (Lamboo Gunian)	60	13	4.6
Lamboo Station	17	5	3.4
Linga	15	4	3.75
Lumukul	12	3	4
Lundja (Red Hill)	25	6	4.1
Mardiwah Loop	250	24	10.4
Marnjal	5	1	5
McGowans Island	4	1	4
Milba	15	3	5

Table 6.2. (Continued)

Mirima	155	16	9.7
Molly Springs	28	1	28
Mud Springs (Ribinyung Dawang)	35	3	7
Munthamar	7	1	7
Ngulwirriwirri	8	1	8
Ngunjuwerrie	25	3	8.3
Nicholson Block	20	4	4
Ningbingi	40	5	8
Nomie Bore	0	1	0
Norton Bore	18	2	9
Nulla Nulla	15	1	15
Nulleywah	60	16	3.9
Oombulgurri	250	58	4.3
Pago	5	2 Sheds	2.5
Quartz Blow	10	2	5
Red Creek	12	1 Shed	12
RB River Junction	5	2 Sheds	5
Turner	10	2	5
Violet Valley	10	4	2.5
Warmun	580	59	9.8
Warrayu	55	8	6.9
Whattarguttabe	10	2	5
Woolah	70	11	6.4
Woolerregerberleng	24	3	8
Wuggubun	30	3	10
Yardgee	16	15	1.06
Yarrunga	25	5	5
Yirralallan (Yirrallem)	15	1	15
Yunggul	8	1	8
Total	2,782	394	7.1

Source: Based on 2001 CHINS and updated by ATSIC community housing survey in 2003

Of course, these data reveal nothing of the quality of housing stock. The 1997 WA Environmental Health Needs Survey (EHNS) provided some measure of this allowing for a more refined (and meaningful) measure of occupancy based on persons per functional dwelling (defined against minimum environmental health criteria). This recalibration produced some excessively high occupancy rates in Northern East Kimberley communities—Mardiwah Loop (14.0), Koongie Park (12.5), Warmun (11.3), Kalumburu (11.1), Oombulgurri (10.4), Flying Foxhole (35), Cockatoo Springs (13.5), Hollow Springs (27), and Nulleywah (40). Unfortunately, the lack of a follow-up survey by the time of writing prevents any assessment of how these rates may have changed in the interim.

More recent measures of the quality of housing stock are provided by the 2001 CHINS that included an assessment of the condition of dwellings owned or managed by Indigenous Housing Organisations. Such dwellings are categorized according to the extent of repairs needed in the following way:

- Minor repairs – repairs of less than $33,000

- Major repairs – repairs of between $33,000 and $100,000

- Replacement – repairs of over $100,000

The 2001 CHINS identified a total of 368 permanent dwellings managed by an Indigenous Housing Organisation in the study region. Of these, 85 (23%) were declared in need of replacement, 58 (16%) were in need of major repair, and all of the remainder were found to be in need of minor repair. These figures for major repair and replacement are in line with estimates made by the Wunan ATSIC Regional Council community housing survey of March 2003 which identified an immediate requirement for 23 new houses, and 125 to be upgraded, although it should be noted that these needs were also seen as contributing to an increase in housing stock to assist in relieving overcrowding. In effect, the indications are that a major component of the Aboriginal-owned and managed housing stock in the region is in need of significant upgrading, while additional dwellings are also required to reduce overcrowding. According to the ATSIC survey, the greatest concentrations of need for extra housing, or housing upgrades are at Warmun (2 new houses required and 30 to be upgraded), Kalumburu (5 new houses required and 24 to be upgraded), and Oombulgurri (1 new house and 39 to be upgraded). The other new housing need identified is scattered across the region in smaller communities such as Woolah, Bell Springs, Emu Creek and Goose Hill.

Housing tenure

Of course, not all Aboriginal households in the study region occupy dwellings that are managed by an Indigenous Housing Organisation. The extent to which other forms of housing tenure are accessed is indicated in Table 6.3 according to whether the dwellings are in one of the three urban areas or in smaller, rural communities. Overall, the majority of Aboriginal dwellings (76%) are rented, whether in town or not. This is a far higher rate of rental than for non-Aboriginal dwellings (44%).

Home ownership

Australia has one of the highest home ownership rates among OECD countries. In line with this, 67% of all Western Australian households in 2001 lived in a dwelling that was either fully owned or mortgaged. Historically, a key factor in this privatisation of housing stock has been a community-wide perception of home ownership as a primary means of enhancing economic status through the provision of secure and, over the longer-term, affordable housing. According to observations made by the ABS, equity accumulated in the family home represents the major part of household wealth for many people (ABS 1998: 154). As well as providing financial security for retirement and unemployment, this equity also yields other economic benefits such as collateral for loans. For all these reasons, home ownership has been, and continues to be, encouraged and promoted by governments.

Given the vital role played by home ownership in the financial developmental cycle of most Australian families, and the attempts by ATSIC over the years to raise the level of Indigenous home ownership, it is striking to note that only 2% of Aboriginal households in the Northern East Kimberley lived in a fully owned dwelling in 2001, while just 3% were resident in a mortgaged dwelling (Table 6.3). By contrast, 41% of non-Aboriginal dwellings in the region were either owned outright or mortgaged. Thus, Aboriginal households in the region remain overwhelmingly dependent on rented accommodation. While, on the one hand, this limits access to the property market for Aboriginal people as a means of improving their financial security, on the other hand it is symptomatic of their relatively low economic status, as well as indicating a cultural focus on communal forms of tenure.

Table 6.3. Aboriginal and non-Aboriginal dwellings by urban/rural location and tenure type: Northern East Kimberley, 2001

	Fully owned	Being purchased	Being rented	Other tenure type	Not stated	Total %
Aboriginal dwellings						
Urban	2.9	3.7	79.3	5.1	9.0	100
Rural	1.2	2.8	70.0	20.2	5.9	100
Total %	2.3	3.4	76.0	10.5	7.9	100
Dwellings (no.)	16	24	538	74	56	708
Non-Aboriginal dwellings						
Urban	19.9	17.3	51.8	5.6	5.5	100
Rural	27.2	25.8	17.1	16.4	13.4	100
Total %	21.4	19.2	44.3	7.9	7.2	100
Dwellings (no.)	295	264	609	109	99	1,376

Source: ABS 2002c

It should also be noted that the non-Aboriginal rate of home ownership is also relatively low by Western Australian (and national) standards. The net effect of this is that the private housing market in the region is a fairly small one. No doubt a key factor in this is the temporary nature of much of the workforce—ironically many individuals who migrate to the East Kimberley for employment probably invest their earnings in property elsewhere, such as Perth. Whatever the case, the result is that only 599 dwellings in the region are privately owned, either outright or under mortgage, with barely 7% of these classified as Aboriginal dwellings. According to the 2001 Census, only 24 Aboriginal dwellings in the region are under mortgage—a remarkably low figure in the context of access to regional wealth accumulation.

Rental housing

According to 2001 Census data, a total of 1,182 dwellings in the region are rented, and Table 6.4 shows the distribution of these by landlord type. Clearly, in towns, Aboriginal people depend much more on State-provided rental housing than do non-Aboriginal people. More than half (55%) of Aboriginal dwellings in Kununurra, Wyndham and Halls Creek are rented from the WA Department of Housing and Works (DHW). This compares to only 21% of non-Aboriginal rental dwellings. The reason for this contrast is that non-Aboriginal residents have a wider range of rental options in town, the most common being to rent from an employer who often provides housing as part of a contract employment package in order to attract workers to the region. The other main source is the private rental market from which Aboriginal households are notably absent. Away from the towns, Aboriginal controlled housing organisations provide almost the entire stock of housing for Aboriginal people, whilst non-Aboriginal renters tend to acquire housing from an employer.

Table 6.4. **Aboriginal and non-Aboriginal rental housing by landlord type: urban and rural areas of the Northern East Kimberley, 2001**

	Private landlord	Real estate agent	State housing	Community housing	Govt. Employer	Other Employer	Other landlord	Total %
	Aboriginal dwellings							
Urban[a]	3.4	5.2	54.6	20.6	13.0	2.3	0.8	100.0
Rural	0.0	0.0	3.3	91.7	3.4	0.0	1.7	100.0
Total %	2.3	3.5	38.1	43.4	9.9	1.6	1.1	100.0
Total dwellings[b]	13	20	215	245	38	18	9	(564)
	Non-Aboriginal dwellings							
Urban	17.3	17.5	21.5	1.1	39.5	2.6	0.5	100.0
Rural	35.3	5.9	5.9	7.8	45.1	0.0	0.0	100.0
Total%	18.8	16.5	20.2	1.6	40.0	2.4	0.5	100.0
Total dwellings	116	102	125	10	195	52	15	(618)

Notes: a. Kununurra, Wyndham, and Halls Creek

b. Total dwellings including landlord type not stated are in parentheses

Source: ABS 2002c

Given the more complex rental options evident in urban settings, it is interesting to compare these census data on rental accommodation in the three East Kimberley towns with tenancy data for June 2001 made available by the DHW. The comparison is provided in Table 6.5. According to the 2001 Census, a total of 544 dwellings in these three towns were rented from the State housing department or from a government employer. In effect, this amounts to the same thing since the DHW manages both sets of housing stock. However, in June 2001, DHW tenancy records revealed a total of 757 dwellings under these forms of tenure—a figure 28% higher than provided by the census. That the DHW figure is correct is undeniable as it is based on actual tenancies on the public record. Thus, something appears amiss with the census data. Two possible explanations suggest themselves.

Table 6.5.   Number of dwellings rented from State housing and government employers in East Kimberley towns: Census and DHW, 2001

Urban centre	State housing		Government employer	
	Census	DHW	Census	DHW
Kununurra	175	271	153	176
Wyndham	60	73	31	39
Halls Creek	96	149	29	49
Total	331	493	213	264

Source: ABS 2002c; Western Australia Department of Housing and Works, 2003

The first possibility is that the census failed to count all such dwellings. While this could be expected to occur to a limited degree, it seems unlikely that it could happen on the scale suggested here, and so it is discounted. The second possibility is that confusion existed either among census interviewers (involved with the Indigenous Enumeration Strategy), census respondents, and census coders, or among all of these, in regard to the proper classification of rental (and possibly of any) tenure. For example, it might be that some households in DHW dwellings either classified themselves, were classified by collectors, or in data processing, as resident in other forms of tenure, with community housing, private rental, and home ownership being the only other options. If the problem is one of misclassification, then the true distribution of dwellings by tenure type is unknown. For this reason, DHW data are preferred for the analysis of urban rental dwellings.

The DHW funding arrangements provide for three types of urban rental outcomes— mainstream public rental, Aboriginal specific rental, and rental dwellings made available to State (or Commonwealth) public servants. Currently, a total of 493 mainstream and Aboriginal-specific public rental houses are available in the three East Kimberley towns— 271 in Kununurra, 149 in Halls Creek and 73 in Wyndham. An additional 264 government employee houses are available. The distribution of mainstream and Aboriginal-specific housing in each town is shown in Table 6.6. Overall, 37% of the State rental housing stock is set aside for exclusive Aboriginal occupancy, although this proportion is much higher in Halls Creek than in the other two towns. However, this does not represent the full complement of Aboriginal public housing tenancies since Aboriginal households are also eligible to apply for and occupy mainstream rental housing. Unfortunately, the precise number that do is unknown since Aboriginal identification in administrative records is incomplete. From the June 2001 tenancy records, at least 54 mainstream rental dwellings (16% of the total) were occupied by self-identified Aboriginal tenants, but DHW estimates that the overall figure could be closer to 50%—indeed, if the Aboriginal share (83%) of applications for mainstream rental accommodation in June 2001 is anything to go by, it could be higher still. Thus, it is possible, though not certain, that as much as two-thirds of State public rental properties (325) are occupied by Aboriginal households.

Table 6.6.   Number of mainstream and Aboriginal-specific DHW rental dwellings in East Kimberley towns, 2003

	Mainstream rental	Aboriginal-specific	Total dwellings	% Aboriginal specific
Kununurra	201	70	271	25.8
Wyndham	58	15	73	20.5
Halls Creek	52	97	149	65.1
Total	311	182	493	36.9

Source: Western Australia Department of Housing and Works, 2003

Turning to the actual DHW tenants data, in February 2003 a total of 488 of the 493 rental dwellings were actually occupied and almost half of these (236, or 48%) were identified in DHW administrative records as Aboriginal dwellings (made up of the Aboriginal-specific rental properties and 54 of the mainstream rental properties). This proportion varied between the three towns, with 41% of the 271 State housing dwellings in Kununurra occupied by Aboriginal households, 59% of the 149 dwellings in Halls Creek, and 57% of those in Wyndham. This overall Aboriginal share of the State housing rental market is noticeably lower than the equivalent census-derived proportion of 63%. However, if the estimate mentioned above is accepted—that 50% of mainstream rental dwellings are occupied by Aboriginal households—then the resulting Aboriginal share of the public rental housing market (68%) is actually very close to the census figure and may provide some confirmation that at least the census proportional share in the form of tenure might be valid.

Clearly, there is imprecision in all this, yet some facts seem assured. First, Aboriginal families have fewer urban housing options than others. Second, their access to urban housing is dependent on continued expansion of State public housing stock, and a guaranteed major share of this. However, if the true size of the regional housing stock by tenure type remains unknown, especially in urban areas, then the estimation of future supply and demand for housing is rendered more difficult and less precise.

Environmental health infrastructure

As with the measurement of housing need, the status of environmental health infrastructure requires a detailed assessment of functionality and adequacy set against agreed normative criteria. However, at the time of writing no secondary source of data was readily available with which to adequately establish change in the findings of the 1997 Environmental Health Survey, nor to establish, in a comprehensive way, the existing status of environmental health infrastructure. The most recent source of data is from the 2001 CHINS, and while this includes information on such issues as water supply, sewerage, drainage and solid waste disposal, this is more in the form of simply noting the existence or otherwise of infrastructure rather than assessing its functionality and adequacy. Likewise, CHINS data do not allow for the proper assessment of activities related to such issues as dust control, animal health and quality of waterways. For example, with regard to dust control, all that is available from the CHINS is the fact that a certain number of permanent dwellings in the region were located on sealed roads. Thus, while this provides some indication of the likely extent of dust mitigation as an issue, it is far from adequate as an indicator of progress.

The idea that Aboriginal community housing and infrastructure should be designed, constructed and maintained to support healthy living practices is now firmly embedded in policy following the pioneering work of Pholeros, Rainow and Torzillo (1993) in the Pitjantjatjara Lands. A total of nine such practices are identified, in descending order of priority in terms of impact on health outcomes: capacity to wash people, wash clothes and bedding, remove waste safely, improve nutrition, reduce crowding, separate people from animals, reduce dust, control temperature, and reduce trauma. Each of these refers to different aspects of the functionality of dwellings and their related infrastructure. For example, if the focus is on improving nutritional standards and practices, then 'healthy home hardware' refers to the provision of adequate facilities to store, prepare and cook food. It also extends to water quality and quantity as a lack of these may lead individuals to purchase bottled water or other beverages, thereby adding to expenditure and increasing reliance on soft drinks and cordials.

The National Indigenous Housing Guide (Commonwealth of Australia 1999) includes a range of detailed design and functionality guidelines to address each of these nine healthy living practices. The key functional area with most guidelines is that involving the supply, usage and removal of water: six of the nine healthy living practices are dependent on these. However, even seemingly obscure health-related housing functions include a wide range of design, maintenance and infrastructural features that require attention (Commonwealth of Australia 1999: 49-57). For example, guidelines for improved nutrition include consideration of the following factors:

- Different ways of cooking: Given often-crowded dwellings and failure of cooking equipment, it is common for many different age groups to share the cooking facilities of a house. At the same time, each group may have a different preference for cooking.

For example, younger people may use a microwave oven; middle-aged people may use a stove or drum oven and barbecue, older people may prefer the ground and a fire for cooking. To this extent, there is a need to consider how many 'kitchens' each house may need.

- Electric cooking: stoves and hotplates. Electric hotplate cooking is one of the major sources of energy use in a house. To control costs, stove timer switches can be installed to cut off power after a set period. It has also been found that solid hotplates are more robust than coil elements.

- Operational fridges: Poorly performing fridges can lead to food spoiling and food poisoning as well as to high energy costs. A number of simple directives can be applied to assist in overcoming these problems, for example ensuring that the fridge is located in a thermally efficient area and that door seals are regularly maintained. However, one problem with fridges in overcrowded households is frequent use, and the only solution here is provide either more fridges or lower density housing.

- Kitchen cleaning and maintenance: The design and detailed specification of the kitchen area, joinery, and appliances can make cleaning easier by reducing cleaning effort and access for insects and vermin.

- Food storage: Low shelves and cupboards are easily accessed by dogs and children, or are unused or used to store non-food items. Consideration should be given to providing high shelves and cupboards and lock-up pantries that are insect-proof and well ventilated.

The main, and most recent, source of data regarding the functionality of dwelling facilities remains the 1997 Environmental Health Needs Survey. For the Wunan ATSIC Region, this revealed that on average some 30% of the dwelling facilities surveyed were absent from dwellings in the region (Table 6.7), the most noticeable being laundry-floor waste outlets. However, if consideration is also given to facilities that are present but not working, then hot water systems were also effectively absent from as many as 48% of dwellings, more than 30% of dwellings had no effective toilet cistern, more than one-third had no effective laundry trough, and 30% had no kitchen sink, bath or shower. Overall, one-third of dwellings was either without facilities, or had facilities that were dysfunctional. Northern East Kimberley communities that stood out as lacking or requiring major repairs to three or more facilities included Oombulgurri, Nulleywah, Glen Hill, Wurrenranginy, Red Hill, Nicholson Camp, Cockatoo Springs, Mud Springs, Darlu Darlu, Crocodile Hole, Nulla Nulla, Baulu Wah, RB River Junction, Yirralallem, Dillon Springs, Woolah, Bow River, Guda Guda, and Molly Springs (Government of Western Australia 1998: 94).

Table 6.7. Functionality of dwelling facilities in Wunan ATSIC Region, 1997

Dwelling facility	% of dwellings with facility absent	% of dwellings with facility working	% of dwellings with facility not working	Total dwellings
External plumbing connection	26.3	70.9	2.8	100.0
On-site sewerage disposal	27.6	70.8	1.6	100.0
Hot water system	30.7	52.6	16.8	100.0
Kitchen sink	26.7	70.0	3.3	100.0
Bath/shower	27.4	70.1	2.5	100.0
Toilet cistern	28.8	67.8	3.4	100.0
Toilet bowl	27.4	70.6	2.0	100.0
Laundry trough	32.2	65.3	2.5	100.0
Laundry waste outlet	41.4	55.0	3.6	100.0

Source: Government of Western Australia 1998:91

However, aside from the constant need to ensure that maintenance funds are available and sufficient to ensure minimum environmental health standards, the main challenge for the future management of housing stock now seems to be to ensure that adequate and planned expansion occurs to accommodate new household formation for a rapidly growing population.

7. Health status

Information on the health status of Aboriginal people is collected as a matter of course in the day-to-day operation of the health care system in the East Kimberley. Couzos and Murray (1999) have summarised the scope, content and quality of health information available for the Kimberley region as a whole, concluding that the implementation of an evidence-based approach to primary health care, including the use of information technology, provides the key to successful health care delivery for the region. At the same time, public access to primary health care data is limited. Thus, while the Ferret data base of the Kimberley Aboriginal Medical Services Council (KAMSC) provides some basis for describing disease prevalences,[1] and while data on Aboriginal birth weights are available from the Kimberley Health Services (KHS), the most comprehensive set of data regarding Aboriginal morbidity, and that which is mostly utilised here, is hospital separations data provided by the WA Department of Health.

Western Australia was the first jurisdiction to include an Indigenous identifier in its hospital statistics. These data are coded to SLA of usual residence and information on the number and diagnosis of hospital separations can therefore be compiled for the East Kimberley region as a whole, though not for the study region.

As is the case with many social indicators, this need for a regional aggregation of statistics is recognised by the Kimberley Regional Aboriginal Health Plan (Atkinson, Bridge and Gray 1999: 36) as an essential requirement for the production of statistically reliable health indicators, given the relatively small size of the populations within the region. While this inevitably involves some loss of geographic detail, it nonetheless enables the compilation of detailed statistics of major morbidity for Aboriginal and non-Aboriginal individuals who indicate the East Kimberley as their usual place of residence. Importantly, in the context of establishing a baseline regional health profile, it also enables the calculation of age-specific rates of hospitalisation, with the proviso that ABS estimated resident population figures and hospital admissions data are assumed to be sufficiently compatible for the former to be employed as a meaningful denominator.

Also available using hospital statistics are comparative data on Aboriginal and non-Aboriginal health status between the East Kimberley and health service regions in the rest of Western Australia. These data, compiled by the Western Australian Department of Health using hospital separations for the period 1994-2000, detail the comparative rates of five conditions that account for 75% of all Aboriginal deaths in Western Australia as a whole—circulatory disease, cancer, respiratory disease, injury and poisoning, and diabetes (Watson, Ejueyitsi, and Codde 2001). As for self-assessed health status, some indication of this is available for the Wunan Regional Council area compared to other regional council areas via the 1994 National Aboriginal and Torres Strait Islander Survey (NATSIS).

Estimation of mortality

The level of mortality provides a proxy measure of health status. While the usual residence of Aboriginal people is recorded in death statistics held by the ABS these are coded only to the SLA level. Thus, in the two SLAs that make up the East Kimberley a total of 502 Aboriginal deaths were recorded between 1991 and 2001—an average of 50 deaths per annum, although the greatest annual number of deaths (61) occurred at the beginning of this period in 1991, and the lowest (36) occurred at the end of the period in 2001, suggesting a decline in death rates over the decade. With these figures of annual deaths, it is possible to calculate a standardised Aboriginal mortality rate for the East Kimberley to account for the quite different age structure of the Aboriginal population and the effect that this might have on the Aboriginal rate compared to the non-Aboriginal rate. Given the relatively small size of the regional Aboriginal population, it is appropriate to apply the indirect method for establishing this (ABS 2002b: 107). This is calculated by applying published age- and sex-specific death rates for the total Australian population (ABS 2002b: 50) to the 2001 regional Aboriginal ERP age/sex distribution. An annual figure for deaths in the East Kimberley is then estimated by averaging recorded deaths over the period 1996-2001 to account for annual variation. This observed figure of 43 Aboriginal deaths for the region is then compared to the expected number (18) derived from the application of the standard age-specific death rates. This produces a standardised mortality ratio for the Aboriginal population of 2.4 indicating that there are more than twice as many Aboriginal deaths in the region than would be expected if the mortality profile observed for the total Australian population applied.

In terms of an indirectly standardised Aboriginal death rate for the East Kimberley, this translates into 15.8 deaths per thousand which is somewhat higher than the equivalent indirect rate of 13.4 deaths per thousand calculated for Indigenous people in Western Australia as a whole (Table 7.1). However, it is significant to note that almost all of this difference is accounted for by the fact that the adjusted death rate for Aboriginal women in the East Kimberley is 60% higher than that recorded for all Indigenous women in Western Australia. Compared to the total non-Indigenous population of Western Australia, overall Aboriginal death rates in the East Kimberley are three times higher. The comparable figure for all Indigenous people in Western Australia is 2.6 times higher. It is not surprising, then, to discover that the median age at death for Aboriginal people in the East Kimberley between 1997 and 2001 was 47 years compared to 53 years for Indigenous people generally in Western Australia, and 78 years for non-Indigenous people (ABS 2002b: 79-80).

Table 7.1.   Indigenous and non-Indigenous indirect standardised death rates[a] for the East Kimberley and Western Australia, 2001

	Male	Female	Total
Indigenous East Kimberley	17.1	14.7	15.8
Indigenous WA	18.3	9.2	13.4
Non-Indigenous WA	N/A[b]	N/A[b]	5.2

Notes: a. Per 1,000

b. N/A = not applicable

Source: Calculated from ABS Deaths registration data, and information in ABS (2002: 35, 86)

Cause of death

Cause of death data are coded using the World Health Organisation (WHO) method of disease classification that follows the 9th Revision, International Classification of Diseases (ICD9) up to July 1999, and the ICD10 classification thereafter. Briefly, the ICD consists of 17 primary disease chapters plus two supplementary classifications dealing with external causes of injury and poisoning, and contact with health services. The ICD10 comprises 21 chapters, incorporating the two previous supplementaries. The two classifications are compared in Table 7.2.

Table 7.2.   ICD9 and ICD10 disease chapters

ICD9	ICD10
Infectious and parasitic diseases	Infectious and parasitic diseases
Neoplasms	Neoplasms
Endocrine, nutritional and metabolic disease and immunity disorders	Diseases of the blood and blood-forming organs and disorders involving the immune system
Diseases of the blood and blood-forming organs	Endocrine, nutritional and metabolic diseases
Mental disorders	Mental and behavioural disorders
Diseases of the nervous system and sense organs	Diseases of the nervous system
Diseases of the circulatory system	Diseases of the eye and adnexa
Diseases of the respiratory system	Diseases of the ear and mastoid process
Diseases of the digestive system	Diseases of the circulatory system
Diseases of the genitourinary system	Diseases of the respiratory system
Complications of pregnancy and childbirth	Diseases of the digestive system
Diseases of the skin	Diseases of the skin and subcutaneous tissue
Diseases of the musculoskeletal system	Diseases of the musculoskeletal system
Congenital anomalies	Diseases of the genitourinary system
Conditions originating in the perinatal period	Pregnancy, childbirth and the puerperium
Symptoms, signs and ill-defined conditions	Conditions originating in the perinatal period
Injury and poisoning;	Congenital malformations, deformations and chromosomal abnormalities
Supplementary classification of factors influencing health status and contact with health services	Symptoms, signs and abnormal clinical and laboratory findings, not elsewhere classified
	Injury and poisoning and consequences of external causes
	External causes of morbidity and mortality
	Factors influencing health status and contact with health services

Table 7.3 shows the proportional distribution of deaths of East Kimberley Aboriginal residents recorded in hospital statistics between 1991 and 2001, with ICD10 categories reclassified by the WA Department of Health to match ICD9. Diseases of the circulatory system (particularly ischaemic heart diseases), and injury and poisoning are the primary causes of death among Aboriginal males, accounting for more than half of all deaths over the 10 year period. These are followed by neoplasms and respiratory diseases. A similar distribution is evident among females, although diabetes-related deaths, and deaths due to genitourinary and digestive diseases feature more prominently.

Standardised death rates

In Western Australia as a whole, the largest rates of Aboriginal deaths are seen in diseases of the circulatory system, respiratory diseases, endocrine disorders (especially diabetes) and injury and poisoning (Watson, Ejueyitsi and Codde 2001). Given that these five disease categories accounted for 75% of such deaths during the 1990s, standardised death rates for each of these conditions have been calculated by the WA Department of Health for each of the health service regions of Western Australia to enable spatial comparison (ibid). One such region is the East Kimberley and results are presented in Table 7.4 to provide comparison between the East and West Kimberley and the State average. Three indicators are provided: the age-standardised rate per thousand population (ASRs); person-years of life lost per death; and the rate ratio between the Aboriginal and non-Aboriginal ASRs recorded for each region.

Table 7.3.   Cause of death for Aboriginal males and females: East Kimberley 1991-2001

ICD9	Males	Females
Infectious and parasitic diseases	2.0	2.7
Neoplasms	10.6	9.2
Endocrine, nutritional, metabolic disease, immunity disorders	3.0	10.8
Diseases of the blood and blood-forming organs	0.3	0.0
Mental disorders	4.0	5.4
Diseases of the nervous system and sense organs	1.7	2.7
Diseases of the circulatory system	29.4	25.4
Diseases of the respiratory system	10.6	4.9
Diseases of the digestive system	3.3	6.5
Diseases of the genitourinary system	3.0	8.1
Complications of pregnancy and childbirth	0.0	0.0
Diseases of the skin	0.3	0.5
Diseases of the musculoskeletal system	0.7	0.5
Congenital anomalies	0.7	3.2
Conditions originating in the perinatal period	1.7	3.2
Symptoms, signs and ill-defined conditions	4.3	3.8
Injury and poisoning	24.8	13.0
All causes	100.0	100.0

Source: WA Department of Health

Table 7.4.   Mortality-related statistics for leading causes of Aboriginal death by selected Western Australian health service region of residence, 1990-1999

	East Kimberley	West Kimberley	Western Australia
	Circulatory diseases		
Age standardised rate	777.9	510.3	580.0
Years of life lost	15.9	16.6	15.6
Rate ratio (region/state)	4.1	3.4	2.3
	Neoplasms		
Age standardised rate	202.6	238.6	213.2
Years of life lost	15.3	12.9	13.2
Rate ratio	2.5	1.2	1.2
	Respiratory diseases		
Age standardised rate	272.6	145.6	175.8
Years of life lost	16.1	22.6	23.4
Rate ratio	6.1	1.2	3.6
	Injury and poisoning		
Age standardised rate	170.6	130.3	125.8
Years of life lost	36.6	32.9	34.4
Rate ratio	3.6	2.0	3.2
	Diabetes		
Age standardised rate	126.0	177.9	137.4
Years of life lost	13.3	11.7	11.5
Rate ratio	23.8	7.8	11.3

Source: Watson, Ejueyitsi and Codde 2001

The East Kimberley stands out as having higher Aboriginal mortality rates for circulatory diseases, respiratory diseases and injury and poisoning (which together account for more than half of all Aboriginal deaths in Western Australia) than those recorded for the West Kimberley and for the State as a whole. However, in terms of relative rates compared to locally recorded non-Aboriginal deaths, the East Kimberley records by far the highest gap in death rates for all five disease categories, especially in regard to diabetes-related deaths. A further measure of the greater burden of mortality in the East Kimberley is provided by the relative person-years of life lost which are greatest in the East Kimberley for all leading causes of death except for respiratory diseases and indicate the generally younger age at death in this region compared to elsewhere in Western Australia.

This profile of mortality confirms the trend towards 'lifestyle' diseases as the primary cause of death first noted by Gracey and Spargo (1987) in their review of the state of Aboriginal health in the Kimberley as a whole from 1970 to 1985. Interestingly, it was this review of the shift in health status that triggered a series of letters to the *Medical*

Journal of Australia (volume 146: 610) regarding the lack of reference to increased alcohol consumption in the region and its likely contribution to morbidity and mortality. Since that time, the development of an aetiological fraction methodology, involving estimation of the proportion of an illness or injury that can be attributed to a risk factor such as alcohol consumption (Holman et al. 1990), has enabled the calculation of alcohol-caused deaths and hospitalisation in Western Australian health service areas for the period 1984-1995 (Unwin et al. 1997).

In the East Kimberley region, a total of 65 deaths were caused by alcohol over the period 1984-1995. This represented approximately 15% of total Aboriginal deaths each year. Of these deaths, 60% were due to alcohol-related diseases such as liver cirrhosis and stroke, and 40% were due to road injuries, assaults and suicide. More importantly, the number of alcohol-caused deaths per head of population was significantly higher in the East Kimberley region (63 per thousand) compared to the State average (20 per thousand), and the observed number of alcohol-caused deaths was also significantly higher than the number expected based on the State rate. Indeed, the East Kimberley had the highest crude rate of alcohol-caused deaths of all health service areas in Western Australia (Unwin et al. 1997).

Hospital separations

Hospital separations data for the Aboriginal and non-Aboriginal usual resident populations of the East Kimberley were obtained for the years 1991 to 2001. Also obtained were principal diagnosis data for all separations coded by ICD9 and ICD10. However, because the data were acquired by calendar year, ICD9 data are anlaysed only for the period 1991 to 1998, and ICD10 data for 2000 and 2001. These data, provided at unit record level, form the basis for compiling a statistical profile of the health status of the regional population. However, because the focus is inevitably on diagnoses of major morbidity (i.e. conditions serious enough to warrant hospitalisation), the data do not provide a full measure of the burden of ill health in the region. An indication of this is provided by analysing clinic-derived data from KAMSC and KHS.

Before considering hospitalisation data in detail, it is important to note that the number of admissions far exceeds the number of individuals admitted. This is obviously because many people are admitted more than once. Among Aboriginal residents of the East Kimberley, for example, a total of 30,908 hospital separations were recorded between 1991 and 2001. However, these separations were generated cumulatively by just 16,547 individuals producing an average of 1.9 separations per patient. The equivalent ratio for non-Aboriginal residents of the East Kimberley over the same period was 1.02 separations per patient, making the Aboriginal ratio twice as high. This gap has remained reasonably stable since 1991, although there has been a slight rise in the ratio of Aboriginal separations to patients, from 1.7 in 1991 to 2.0 in 2001. However, it is difficult to interpret this rise in the ratio of separations to patients as it may reflect a number of factors: that people are now more sick and therefore require more treatment; that access to the hospital system has improved; or that local health staff are now more inclined to refer cases to hospital. Which of these holds true has not been determined.

An indication of the age pattern of hospital admissions is provided in Table 7.5, which shows the hospital separation rate for Aboriginal and non-Aboriginal males and females in the East Kimberley by five-year age group for the period 2000-01 using the 2001 ERP as a denominator. Figure 7.1 illustrates the pattern separately for Aboriginal males and females. Several stages of morbidity are apparent based on prevailing rates at different ages. First, high rates of hospitalisation are evident among both male and female infants aged 0-4 years, especially among Aboriginal infants as indicated by the relatively high rate ratios. Separation rates then fall away gradually up to the age group 20-24 for Aboriginal males, and 15-19 for females owing to relatively high levels of teenage pregnancy. Beyond the age of 30 years hospitalisation rates for Aboriginal males and females are high, both absolutely and relative to their non-Aboriginal counterparts despite a tendency for all rates to increase with advancing age. In the oldest age groups over 60 years, Aboriginal rates are exceedingly high for both males and females owing largely to high demand for renal dialysis.

Table 7.5.   Age-specific hospital separation rates[a]: Aboriginal and non-Aboriginal residents of the East Kimberley, 2000-2001

	Aboriginal (1)		Non-Aboriginal (2)		Rate Ratio (1/2)	
	Males	Females	Males	Females	Males	Females
0-4	1324.3	1105.7	336.5	270.8	3.9	4.1
5-9	408.6	258.6	218.9	154.7	1.9	1.7
10-14	235.5	317.4	217.4	103.7	1.1	3.1
15-19	245.6	1030.5	450.0	451.2	0.5	2.3
20-24	492.1	1327.4	269.4	419.4	1.8	3.2
25-29	609.4	1263.2	224.2	542.6	2.7	2.3
30-34	1508.6	2200.0	305.1	554.3	4.9	4.0
35-39	1158.5	1091.8	359.7	409.3	3.2	2.7
40-44	1055.6	1754.8	395.6	412.7	2.7	4.3
45-49	1556.5	1910.6	385.6	424.4	4.0	4.5
50-54	1642.0	1883.7	432.8	327.0	3.8	5.8
55-59	1437.5	1985.5	673.2	650.6	2.1	3.1
60-64	2551.0	661.0	632.1	244.9	4.0	2.7
65+	4960.0	4465.1	680.7	644.7	7.3	6.9
Total	882.1	1144.0	368.2	402.2	2.4	2.8

Note: a. Per 1,000 population

Figure 7.1. Age-specific hospital separation rates: Aboriginal male and female residents of the East Kimberley, 2000–2001

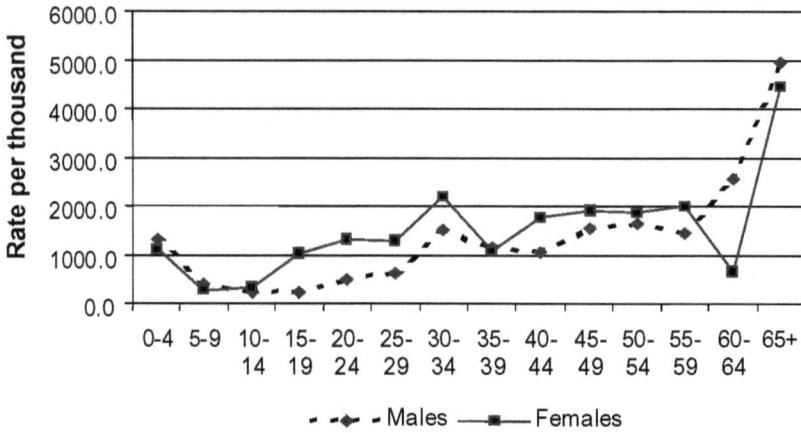

Hospitalisation diagnoses

In profiling the nature of morbidity as defined by principal disease diagnosis, data for all hospital separations (including repeat separations) are utilised. This is because individuals can, and often are, admitted to hospital more than once, but for quite different reasons. Table 7.6 shows the distribution of separations by ICD10 category for male and female Aboriginal residents of the East Kimberley over the period 2000-2001. More than 6,000 such separations were recorded over this two-year period, 56% of them due to females. Over the 10-year period between 1991 and 2001 the total number of Aboriginal separations amounted to 30,908 suggesting a fairly stable average of around 3,000 separations per annum. In 2001, this represented an annual separation rate of around 500 per thousand.

The first point to note is the quite distinct difference between male and female causes of hospitalisation. Almost one-fifth of separations among females were classified as complications of pregnancy and childbirth, although 14% of these involved normal spontaneous deliveries. While this somewhat distorts comparison, it is apparent that males and females share a similar morbidity profile. Thus, infectious disease, diseases of the circulatory system, skin diseases, injury and poisoning, and dialysis are common reasons for hospital admission among both sexes. At the same time, different conditions appear to be more prevalent among males (diseases of the nervous system, the respiratory system, skin diseases and injury and poisoning), and among females (diseases of the genitourinary system).

Table 7.6. Hospital separations by cause: Aboriginal residents of the East Kimberley, 2000–2001

ICD10 disease chapter	Separations Males (no.)	Separations Females (no.)	Proportion of separations Males (%)	Proportion of separations Females (%)
Infectious	156	184	5.9	5.4
Neoplasms	34	38	1.3	1.1
Endocrine/nutritional	7	23	0.3	0.7
Blood and related organs	43	73	1.6	2.1
Mental disorders	109	101	4.1	3.0
Nervous system	118	47	4.4	1.4
Eye and adnexa	40	22	1.5	0.6
Ear and mastoid process	49	51	1.8	1.5
Circulatory system	124	118	4.7	3.5
Respiratory system	376	403	14.2	11.8
Digestive system	143	138	5.4	4.0
Skin	162	124	6.1	3.6
Musculoskeletal system	63	72	2.4	2.1
Genitourinary system	47	144	1.8	4.2
Pregnancy, childbirth	0	673	0.0	19.7
Perinatal conditions	34	43	1.3	1.3
Congenital malformations	16	5	0.6	0.1
Symptoms n.e.c.	144	181	5.4	5.3
Injury and poisoning	467	451	17.6	13.2
Health service contact	524	517	19.7	15.2
Total (excluding dialysis)	2,248	3,053	84.6	89.6
Total (including dialysis)	2,656	3,408	100.0	100.0

These contrasts and similarities between male and female morbidity are made clearer in Figure 7.2 using ICD9 data for the period 1991–1998 with female separations for complications of pregnancy and childbirth (ICD9 Chapter X1) omitted. Comparison with the morbidity profile of male and female non-Aboriginal residents of the region is provided in Figure 7.3. The non-Aboriginal morbidity profile is broadly equivalent with injury and poisoning, diseases of the respiratory and circulatory systems, and factors influencing contact with health services looming large, but clear contrasts also exist. For example, diseases of the respiratory system are far more prominent among Aboriginal males and females, as are infectious diseases, while Aboriginal females are far more likely to be hospitalised for diseases of the nervous system, and for injury and poisoning than are their non-Aboriginal counterparts.

Figure 7.2.   Male and female Aboriginal hospital separations by ICD9 chapter:[a] East Kimberley, 1991–1998

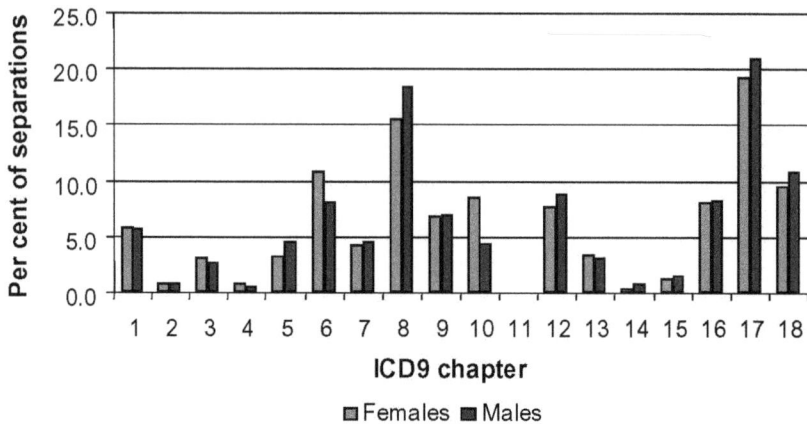

Figure 7.3.   Male and female non-Aboriginal hospital separations by ICD9 chapter: East Kimberley, 1991–1998

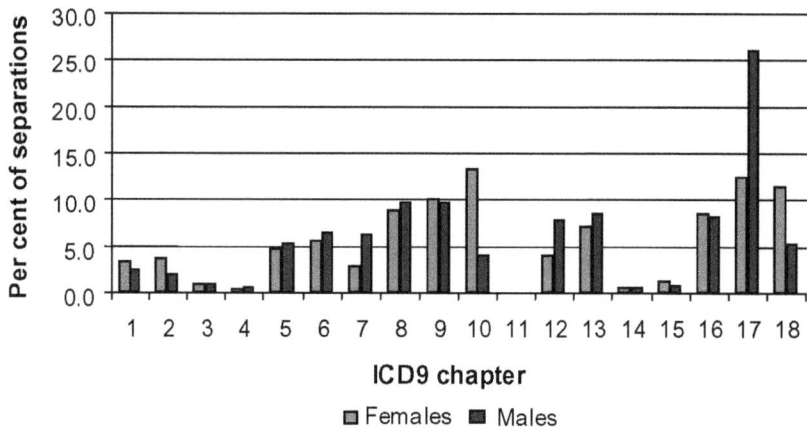

Note: a. Excludes Chapter 11: complications of pregnancy and childbirth

Key to Figures 7.2 and 7.3:

1. Infectious and parasitic diseases. 2. Neoplasms. 3. Endocrine, nutritional and metabolic disease and immunity disorders. 4. Diseases of the blood and blood-forming organs; 5. Mental disorders. 6. Diseases of the nervous system and sense organs. 7. Diseases of the circulatory system. 8. Diseases of the respiratory system. 9. Diseases of the Digestive system. 10. Diseases of the genitourinary system. 11. Complications of pregnancy and childbirth. 12. Diseases of the skin. 13. Diseases of the musculoskeletal system. 14. Congenital anomalies. 15. Conditions originating in the perinatal period. 16. Symptoms, signs and ill-defined conditions. 17. Injury and poisoning. 18. Supplementary classification of factors influencing health status and contact with health services.

Standardised separation rates

Watson, Ejueyitsi and Codde (2001) have calculated standardised separation rates for the five leading causes of Aboriginal death in Western Australia. As with the relative death rates shown earlier, these are presented in Table 7.7 for the East and West Kimberley and the State average. This shows that the age-standardised Aboriginal morbidity rate is markedly higher in the East Kimberley for circulatory diseases, respiratory diseases, and injury and poisoning compared to those recorded in the West Kimberley and Western Australia as a whole. However, as was the case with relative death rates, the rate ratio with non-Aboriginal morbidity is highest in the East Kimberley across all the disease categories.

Once again an aetiological fraction methodology can be applied to hospital separations data to estimate the proportion of illnesses and injuries attributable to alcohol consumption (Unwin et al. 1997). These are shown in Table 7.8 using all separations from the East Kimberley for the period 1993-1995. Overall, one-third of alcohol-related separations were manifest as diseases, mostly alcoholism, while most such separations presented as injuries due largely to assault. Of related interest is the length of time spent in hospital as a consequence, together with the share of the cost of hospital care due to alcohol-related conditions. According to Unwin et al. (1997), the average cost of alcohol-caused hospitalisation in the East Kimberley in 1993-95 was $402,747 equivalent to $46 per capita. This was much higher than the state average of only $15 per head, and slightly above the West Kimberley figure of $44, making the average cost of alcohol-related hospitalisation in the East Kimberley the highest for any health service area in Western Australia at that time. As shown in Table 7.8, much of this cost burden was due to assaults and alcoholism.

Table 7.7. **Standardised hospital separation rates for select ICD9 categories by Western Australian health service region of residence, 1990–1999**

	East Kimberley	West Kimberley	Western Australia
	Circulatory diseases		
Age standardised rate	44.2	36.3	41.3
Rate ratio	6.0	2.2	2.2
	Neoplasms		
Age standardised rate	8.2	10.6	10.6
Rate ratio	1.7	0.7	0.6
	Respiratory diseases		
Age standardised rate	101.8	91.6	82.7
Rate ratio	6.4	3.7	5.2
	Injury and poisoning		
Age standardised rate	96.8	81.9	69.6
Rate ratio	4.3	2.7	3.6
	Diabetes		
Age standardised rate	10.6	12.2	13.2
Rate ratio	21.2	11.1	12.0

Source: Watson, Ejueyitsi, and Codde 2001

Table 7.8.   Hospital separations due to alcohol-related conditions: Total population of the East Kimberley, 1993–1995

Alcohol-related conditions	No. of hospital admissions	Average length of stay (days)	% of alcohol-caused cost
Liver cirrhosis	17	5.4	3.3
Alcoholism	160	3.0	17.3
Cancers	0	0	0.0
Stroke	7	10.3	2.6
Other related diseases	68	3.0	7.5
Road injuries	61	5.2	11.5
Falls	70	4.4	11.1
Suicide	6	3.3	0.7
Assaults	314	3.3	38.3
Other related injuries	26	8.2	7.7
Total	729	3.8	100.0

Source: Unwin et al. 1997

Unfortunately, the Unwin et al. study does not differentiate Aboriginal from non-Aboriginal separations. To provide some measure of the differential impact of alcohol on morbidity among East Kimberley residents, an assessment of alcohol-related conditions by Aboriginality was extracted from the separations data obtained from the WA Department of Health over the longer period from 1991-1998, although with reference only to the 17 primary chapters of ICD9 and therefore excluding the supplementary classification of external causes of injury and poisoning. Over this period, a total of 1,265 diagnosed hospital separations due to alcohol-related conditions were recorded among Aboriginal residents of the East Kimberley comprising 5.5% of all Aboriginal separations. The equivalent figures for non-Aboriginal residents were 243 and 3.3%.

Stages of morbidity

Using ICD10 primary diagnosis data for hospital separations by 5-year age group, it is possible to characterise broad stages of major morbidity through significant stages of the life cycle. This is done in a series of charts that show age-specific separation rates for the Aboriginal population of the East Kimberley according to select ICD10 disease categories. The selection of disease categories is based on those shown to be most prevalent in Table 7.3. In considering these charts, certain customised age groups are worth bearing in mind from the point of view of impact planning. These include the infant and pre-schooling age group (0-4 years), the years of compulsory schooling age group (5-14 years), the years of school-to-work transition age group (15-24 years), the years of family formation and employment age group (25-44 years), the years of family dissolution age group (45-64 years), and an aged category of those over 65 years, although arguably this latter category could be set at a much earlier cut-off point given the evidence for premature ageing in the context of high levels of Aboriginal adult mortality and morbidity (Divarakan-Brown 1985).

Infectious diseases

Figure 7.4 shows the prevalence of infectious diseases in the East Kimberley by 5-year age group. Clearly, these are most prominent among infants, with a rapid drop-off in school years and among young adults, though with some rise again in middle age and older years. Among infants, by far the most common infectious diseases are intestinal, presenting mostly as gastroenteritis, followed by scabies. Among older people, bacterial and viral infections are the more common cause of hospitalisation.

Figure 7.4.   Age-specific Aboriginal separation rates for infectious diseases: East Kimberley, 2000–2001

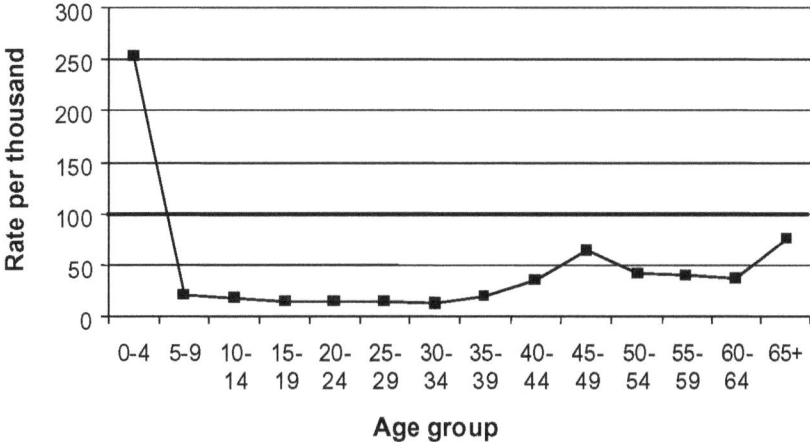

Diseases of the circulatory system

Hypertensive diseases, ischaemic heart diseases, pulmonary heart diseases, heart failure, and cerebrovascular diseases are all common reasons for hospitalisation among Aboriginal residents of the East Kimberley. Manifestation of these diseases commences in the early 30s and rises steadily through middle ages to reach prominence at older ages (Figure 7.5). With relatively high rates of over 100 per thousand by age 40, diseases of the circulatory system are a primary contributor to the overall profile of high adult morbidity observed in the region.

Figure 7.5.   Age-specific Aboriginal separation rates for diseases of the circulatory system: East Kimberley, 2000–2001

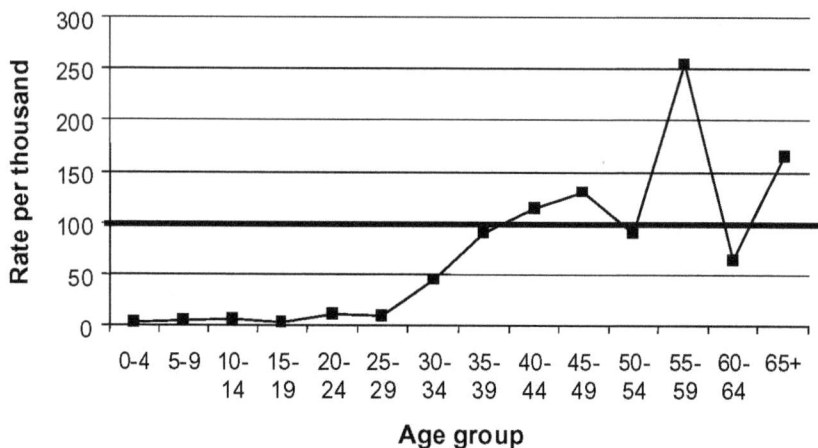

Diseases of the respiratory system

Very high rates of hospitalisation of 400 per thousand due to respiratory disease are evident among infants (Figure 7.6). These range across the disease classification, but especially prominent among infants are acute upper respiratory infections, influenza, pneumonia and asthma. As with diseases of the circulatory system, those of the respiratory system increase in prevalence in middle age over 35 years reaching a plateau of relatively high rates over 200 per thousand among the over 50s.

Figure 7.6.   Age-specific Aboriginal separation rates for diseases of the respiratory system: East Kimberley, 2000–2001

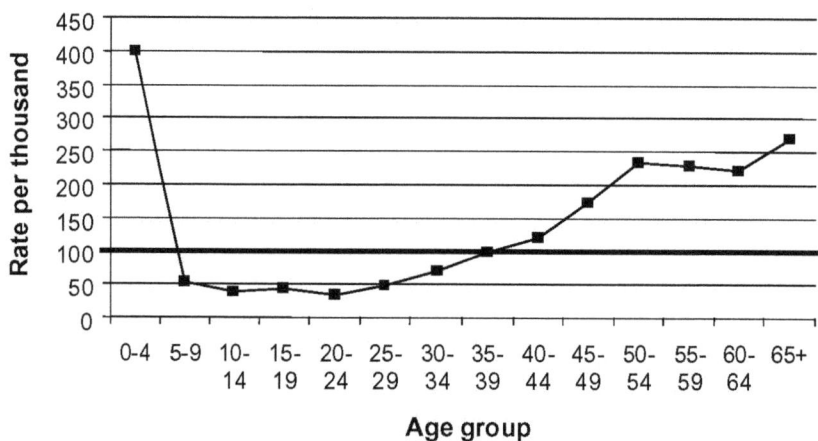

Diseases of the digestive system

Hospital separations for digestive diseases, which often reflect poor nutrition, are relatively absent among infants and youth, but rise suddenly in the late 20s age group and remain at a fairly steady rate thereafter at around 90 per thousand (Figure 7.7). Prominent diagnoses include diseases related to dental problems (especially at younger ages), gastritis, and diseases of the gallbladder and pancreas. Interestingly, diseases of the liver represent only a minor share of hospital diagnoses.

Figure 7.7.   Age-specific Aboriginal separation rates for diseases of the digestive system: East Kimberley, 2000–2001

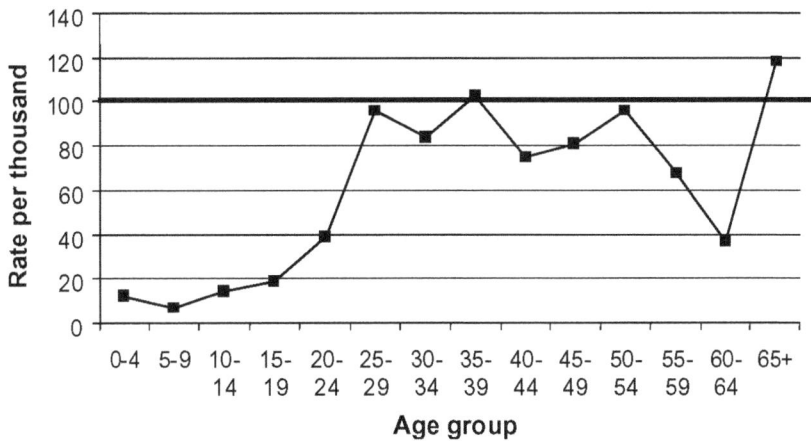

Diseases of the skin and subcutaneous tissue

Skin infections such as impetigo and abscesses are diagnosed relatively frequently among infants, although rates fall through the teen years (Figure 7.8). However, hospitalisation rates rise again through the young adult ages to plateau at around 80 per thousand among those aged between 30 and 50 years, before a further increase among the over 50s. Of interest is a rise in the incidence of cellulitis with increasing age, for which one known risk factor is diabetes.

Figure 7.8. Age-specific Aboriginal separation rates for diseases of the skin and subcutaneous tissue: East Kimberley, 2000–2001

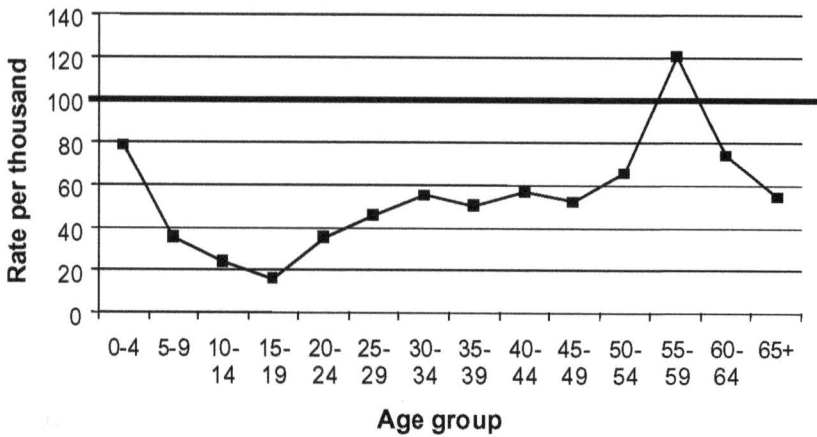

Injury and poisoning

Hospitalisation for reasons of injury and poisoning is very much a feature of young adult to middle age groups, with relatively low rates among children and older people (Figure 7.9). Despite this age variation, however, the primary diagnoses are reasonably similar across all ages and mostly involve injuries, wounds, fractures, and burns to various parts of the anatomy, along with complications of trauma and surgical and medical care. From Table 7.8, it is apparent that road injuries, falls, and assaults contribute substantially to this particular morbidity profile.

Figure 7.9. Age-specific Aboriginal separation rates for injury, poisoning and certain other consequences of external causes: East Kimberley, 2000–2001

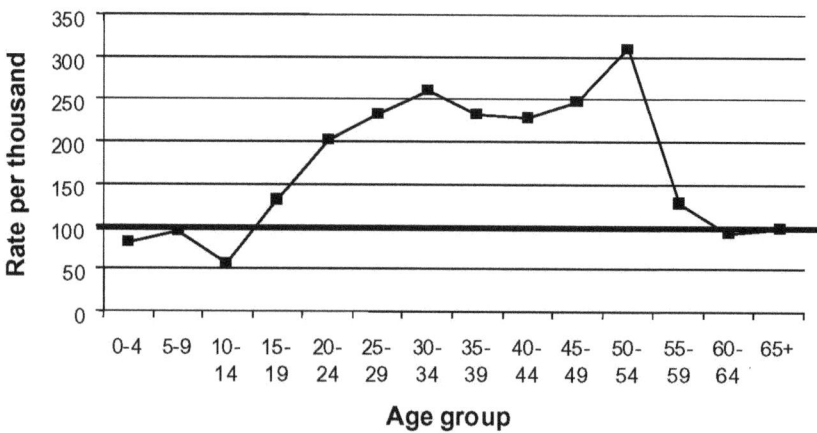

Dialysis

Among separations due to factors influencing health status and contact with health services, the need for regular attendance at regional centres for renal dialysis is a major factor leading to very high separation rates. As shown in Figure 7.10, dialysis separation rates commence rising at a relatively early age between 15 and 19 years and despite considerable fluctuation from one age group to the next, the trend line displays a general increase with age, with the rate of increase peaking around the mid 30s by which time separation rates are typically in excess of 300 per thousand due to the need for repeated treatment.

Figure 7.10. Age-specific Aboriginal separation rates for dialysis: East Kimberley, 2000–2001

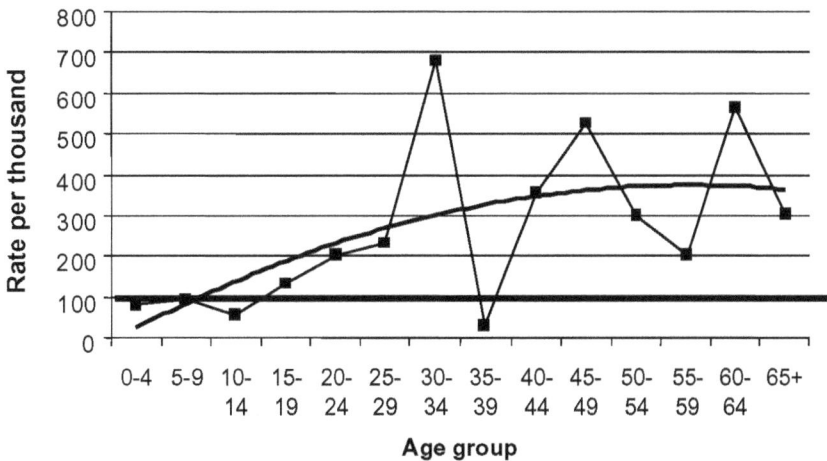

Primary health status

As part of their contribution to the East Kimberley Impact Assessment Project, Gracey and Spargo (1987) surveyed the change in health status of Aboriginal people across the Kimberley over the 15 years from 1970 to 1985—in effect the period leading up to and just beyond the commencement of mining at Argyle. Their main observation was to declare the almost complete eradication of leprosy and a suppression in the prevalence of preventible infectious diseases, although they were careful to point out that rates for such conditions as enteric disease, chronic ear disease, and trachoma were still relatively high. Alongside these improvements, they also noted the onset of a 'new' disease profile associated with urbanisation and lifestyle changes and reflected in increased prevalence of obesity, hypertension, diabetes and coronary heart disease, as well as in a rising incidence of sexually transmitted diseases, alcoholism and related disorders, and in injury and poisoning consequent on motor vehicle accidents and violence (Gracey and Spargo 1987: 16).

As a follow-up study, Gracey, Gunzburg and Spargo (1989) conducted a two-week medical survey of Warmun community and gathered information from 136 adults representing 93% of the adult population aged over 20 years. They found a high level of ill health in the population. Overall, 65% of adults showed signs of previous trachoma, 43% had evidence of respiratory tract disease (mostly bronchitis and pneumonia), 27% had suffered from leprosy and had been treated, 19% had high blood pressure, and 29% had urinary tract infections (mostly women). There was a relatively low rate of documented heart disease (15%), but high rates of sexually transmitted disease (STD), with 35% having syphilis and 21% gonorrhoea. While similar community-base data were not available for the present study, it is interesting to compare these findings with the various profiles of morbidity available for the wider region from hospital separations as discussed above, and from clinic presentations data shown in Table 7.9.

Table 7.9. Notification of main infectious diseases by Kimberley postcode area, 2002

	Kununurra	Wyndham	Halls Creek	Kimberley
Crytosporidiosis	4.4	1.6	3.1	3.8
Giardiasis	13.3	31.7	10.4	14.6
Ross River virus	14.1	10.0	0.0	4.0
Salmonella	7.2	11.7	5.8	6.3
Chlamydia	14.1	15.0	26.0	23.8
Gonorrhoea	14.9	5.0	38.8	27.8
Syphilis	18.5	1.6	9.0	6.0
Total notifications	248	60	423	1,736
% of total notifications	86.5	76.6	93.1	86.3
STDs summary % of total	47%	22%	74%	57.6%

Source: *Kimberley Public Health Unit Bulletin,* Issue 33, February 2003

Clearly, many of the conditions that were described for Warmun, and for the Kimberley in general in the mid-1980s remain prevalent today in the form of enteric diseases, respiratory diseases, high blood pressure, urinary tract infection and sexually transmitted diseases. Compared to the Gracey et al. observations, it would appear that heart disease is now more prevalent, while conditions such as trachoma, and certainly leprosy, far less so. Diabetes would also appear to be more prevalent if the lack of any reference to this condition in the 1980s Warmun study is any guide, although the high rates of sexually transmitted disease noted in the 1980s appear to have risen further, with STDs accounting for as much as 47% of all infectious disease notifications in the Kununurra postcode area in 2002, for 22% in the Wyndham area, and 74% in the Halls Creek area.

Further insight into current disease prevalence in the Northern East Kimberley is provided by the Ord Valley Aboriginal Health Service (OVAHS) Ferret database for regular clients resident in Kununurra and surrounding outstations as at January 2003. Table 7.10 refers to those aged 20 years and over and indicates the number of active cases by disease type and their prevalence out of a total of 918 clients in rising rank order of prevalence. These data underline the impact of so-called 'lifestyle' diseases on the current health profile of the regional population. The most prevalent reported include diabetes, high blood pressure, high cholesterol and kidney failure, all of which are related to dietary factors, alcohol consumption, lack of exercise and smoking. Sexually transmitted disease also appears again as a major component of current regional morbidity.

Table 7.10.   Disease prevalences among OVAHS regular clients aged over 20 years: January 2003

	Active cases	Prevalence (per thousand)
Chronic ear disease	2	2.2
End stage renal failure	2	2.2
Hepatitis B	5	5.4
Major mental illness	5	5.4
Epilepsy	8	8.7
Cirrhosis/chronic liver disease	10	10.8
Rheumatic heart disease	11	11.9
Rheumatic fever	12	12.3
Thyroid disease	15	16.3
Pap smear abnormality (high)	22	23.9
Pap smear inconclusive	24	26.1
Anaemia	24	26.1
Chronic heart disease	25	27.2
Alcohol – unsafe use	28	30.5
Respiratory–chronic	34	37.0
Chronic renal impairment	37	40.3
Hyperlipidaemia	50	54.4
Asthma	56	61.0
Pap smear abnormality (low)	62	67.5
Proteinuria	90	98.0
Hypertension	92	100.2
Diabetes	105	114.4
Syphilis	106	115.5

Source: Ferret database, Ord Valley Aboriginal Health Service, Kununurra

Child health

Many of the conditions that contribute to the overall profile of Aboriginal adult morbidity and mortality in the Northern East Kimberley and wider region have their antecedents in poor childhood and maternal nutrition. Measures of weight and height gain provide a standard public health measure of poor nutrition by yielding estimates of children who are underweight (for age) and those not growing well (below average weight for age). Unfortunately, according to the KHS, such data for the East Kimberley is very incomplete due to the number of short term/relieving staff who do not always appreciate the importance of data collection. According to KAMSC, added to this is the problem of slow computer links in the East Kimberley that induce health staff to enter no more data than absolutely necessary. Even though 'failure to thrive' data is considered a high priority, information on this is patchy at best, and consequently difficult to translate into systematic and reliable population rates.

However, one indicator which is available and that reflects increased risk of neonatal and infant morbidity and mortality is birth weight. This also reflects a number of preconditions including prematurity, poor maternal nutrition, high alcohol intake and smoking. In 2002, there were 92 Aboriginal births recorded at Kununurra hospital with a mean weight of 3,190 grams. While this is notably lower than the average weight of 3,444 grams for non-Aboriginal births at Kununurra in the same year, it is slightly above the mean weight of all Indigenous births in Western Australia in 1999, which was 3,078 grams (Nassar and Sullivan 2002). However, a more useful measure is provided by the prevalence of low birth weights indicated by the proportion of live births with a weight of less than 2,500 grams. This data is available for births at Kununurra in 2002 and reveals that 14% of all Aboriginal live births in that year were less than 2,500 grams (as was the case for Aboriginal births in Western Australia as a whole) compared to only 4% of all non-Aboriginal births. It is important to note that these relativities extend into childhood morbidity and beyond, and they reflect greater failure to thrive among Aboriginal children. For example, 31% of children aged 5 years and under who were registered as regular clients with the Ord Valley Aboriginal Health Service in 2003 were classified as 'children at risk'—an assessment that includes failure to thrive.

It has long been recognised that poor diet and nutritional status are strongly associated (along with other risk factors) with a variety of chronic, preventable, and non-communicable diseases that are highly prevalent in Aboriginal communities. Primary among these in later life are cardiovascular disease and diabetes, but malnutrition also forms part of the general complex of reduced resistance to infectious and other diseases and may engender its own morbidity profile. Not surprisingly, public health programs, especially those targeted at improving health outcomes among Aboriginal people, increasingly identify improved nutrition as an essential intervention. A prerequisite to successful intervention, however, is the identification of structural impediments to improved nutrition, many of which are behavioural and economic in nature, including patterns of household expenditure, store management, and food prices (Taylor and Westbury 2000).

In terms of overall morbidity, nutritional diseases loom large in the East Kimberley and therefore successful intervention in this area has considerable potential to assist in raising health status. Diet-related diseases (including dialysis) can be separately identified using appropriate ICD codes (Lester 1994: 223). If separations for dialysis are included, such diseases accounted for as much as 17% of all East Kimberley Aboriginal hospital separations between 1991 and 2001. If separations for dialysis are excluded, they accounted for 11% of all separations. The main diet-related diseases included intestinal infections, diabetes mellitus, non-infective gastroenteritis, ischaemic and other heart disease, and symptoms concerning nutrition, metabolism and development.

Part of the difficulty in improving dietary intake, and thereby raising nutritional status in East Kimberley Aboriginal communities, is the relatively high cost of foodstuffs compared to other parts of Western Australia, and in relation to low regional household incomes. Nutritionists from the Kimberley Public Health Unit have for a number of years organised the Kimberley Market Basket Survey to establish the relative fortnightly cost of feeding a family of five in various parts of the Kimberley compared to Perth, using a 'standard' basket of basic foodstuffs and household essentials. Results from this survey for the period 1992-1999 are shown in Table 7.11 for the three towns of the East Kimberley, for an average of selected East Kimberley communities (including Oombulgurri, Turkey Creek Roadhouse, and Wungkul from within the study region), for an average of selected West Kimberley communities, and for Broome and Perth. Also shown are the prices in East Kimberley community stores expressed as a ratio of prices in Perth.

Table 7.11.   Average fortnightly cost of food and non-food items ($): Kimberley Market Basket Survey, 1992-1999[a]

	1992	1993	1994	1995	1996	1997	1998	1999
Perth	252	273	280	307	304	305	305	356
Broome	311	360	374	412	364	375	382	413
Halls Creek	427	395	390	387	415	431	466	478
Wyndham	333	373	360	366	389	405	420	460
Kununurra	N/A[b]	359	341	376	385	366	386	409
West Kimberley	416	435	438	458	472	472	462	472
East Kimberley	463	483	489	514	501	509	541	560
E. Kim/Perth Ratio	1.8	1.8	1.7	1.7	1.6	1.7	1.8	1.6

Notes: a. From 1999, the Kimberley Market Basket Survey was renamed as the Western Australian Aboriginal Communities Stores' Survey

b. N/A = not applicable

Notwithstanding methodological problems in comparing process between places and over time due to variable coverage, and some averaging for missing items, it appears that prices in the East Kimberley, both in communities and in towns, were consistently higher than prices in the West Kimberley and in Broome by a factor of between 10% and 20%. However, the price differential between East Kimberley community stores and Perth was less equivocal with prices ranging from 60% to 80% higher. One solution to reducing such differentials that has been attempted elsewhere by organisations such as the Arnhem Land Progress Association in the Northern Territory, and Anangu Winkiku Stores in South Australia, is the integration and pooling of store management, policies, transport and supply to access bulk purchase discounts (Taylor and Westbury 2000: 28). Such an option has been canvassed by Wunan ATSIC Regional Council for stores in the East Kimberley with some evidence of support but only if decision making remains with individual managers and communities (BKR Walker Wayland 2001).

The other main childhood disease identified in clinic presentations data is chronic ear disease. In 2003, the OVAHS reported a prevalence rate for chronic ear disease of 8% among its 319 regular clients aged 0-5 years. More serious cases of ear disease result in hospitalisation and in 2000-2001, 100 hospital separations from the East Kimberley were diagnosed as diseases of the ear and mastoid process—more than one quarter of these (27%) involved infants, and as many as 80% were for children under the age of 15 years. For the most part, these separations were diagnosed as otitis externa, otitis media, and perforated eardrum.

Health-related quality of life assessment

The extent to which policy interventions are perceived by individuals to effect an improvement in their quality of life is an emergent concern of health policy in Australia, including in regard to Aboriginal people (Brady, Kunitz and Nash 1997). This concern with measures of health that go beyond objective indicators such as morbidity and mortality is based on the recognition that a full assessment of health status should include physical, mental, social, and spiritual dimensions.

A more practical reason is the need for timely assessment of health interventions which may take a long time to translate into changes in conventional indicators of health status such as those compiled using hospitals separations data, especially at the whole-of-population level. Furthermore, it appears that many health treatments, while effective from a biomedical point of view, may actually compromise quality of life. An example is the treatment of end-stage renal disease, which requires the relocation of rural-based patients into towns for dialysis. In the East Kimberley context, this involves moving far from home to Broome or Perth with attendant difficulties in sustaining the comfort and care provided by family members. Individuals also have to adjust to living in an unfamiliar and institutional environment and financial hardships can be incurred, especially in terms of the wider caring responsibilities of family groups. All these factors can make treatment costly in terms of loss of quality of life, and may make non-compliance (and associated shortened life expectancy) preferable to adherence (Willis 1995).

In an attempt to discover individuals' perceptions of their own health-related quality of life (QOL) in a routine way which can be repeated over time to monitor changes in condition, and produce results that are comparable with other groups, a number of standard instruments have been developed. These attempt to cover a number of QOL-related aspects of health, such as physical functioning, emotional wellbeing and support from family. Some of these instruments, such as the Medical Outcomes Trust Short Form 36 (SF-36) and its companion question on self-assessed health status within the main sample of the National Health Survey (NHS), are regularly used in Australia and are considered to be reliable, valid, and responsive to changes in clinical condition. While the same conclusion has been drawn for Indigenous people in urban settings, this cannot be claimed from data for remote communities where mainstream conceptions of quality of life and links to health status are indeterminate and poorly understood (ABS/NCEPH 1997).

As far as the East Kimberley is concerned such population-based assessments are scarce and, to date, derive solely from the application of self-assessed health status questions in the 1994 NATSIS. This used the standard global question asking, 'In general, would you say that your health is excellent, very good, good, fair or poor?' As in most other remote regions of Northern Australia, answers to this question in the East Kimberley appear somewhat counter-intuitive. For example, although 50 per cent of respondents in the Wunan ATSIC Region reported an illness in the two weeks prior to the NATSIS, and 25% reported one or more long-term illnesses, 48% considered themselves to be in very good or excellent health, while just one per cent described their health as being poor (ABS 1996: 17-19). Although this raises an obvious question of why people rate their health as good or excellent when the statistics show it to be otherwise, no research is available from the East Kimberley to provide an answer.

Note:

1. Such data were forthcoming from the Ord Valley Aboriginal Health Service in Kununurra, but not from the Yuri Yangi Medical Service in Halls Creek.

8. Regional involvement in the Western Australian criminal justice system

At the 1994 NATSIS, an estimated 35% of Aboriginal people aged 13 years and over in the East Kimberley reported that they had been arrested by police in the previous five years (ABS 1996: 70). This was by far the highest arrest rate reported out of all the ATSIC Regions in the country (only one other region, Ceduna with 32%, reported a rate over 30%). In Western Australia as a whole the rate was 25%, while rates for the West Kimberley were 25% in Broome and 16% for Derby. More recently, a survey based on a wide sample of Kimberley Aboriginal communities and aimed at identifying major justice issues as perceived by residents of the region, found that 77% of Aboriginal respondents knew someone who had made a court appearance, with over half of these being family members (Colmar Brunton WA & Colmar Brunton Social Research 2002: 68-9).

The fact is, interaction with the police, and subsequently with the courts and various custodial institutions, has become so pervasive as to form a major part of the social and economic system with which many Aboriginal individuals, families and households in the East Kimberley find themselves encumbered. While this landscape of recidivism may be seen as providing some measure of social dysfunction within the region, without a clear understanding of precisely what a notion of dysfunction might constitute in this context, it is more usefully viewed in its more literal sense as the extent to which individuals transgress the criminal code. This is the manner in which the involvement of the regional population with the criminal justice system is dealt with here.

Having said that, one relationship between recidivism and the regional society and economy that is reasonably apparent concerns the degree to which past and present convictions and interaction with police, courts and prisons, influence individual chances of participating successfully in the regional economy. Criminologists have long been interested in the relationship between unemployment and crime. However, they have spent much more time examining the effect of unemployment on criminal behaviour, than on the effect of a criminal conviction on an individual's employment prospects (Hunter and Borland 1999). By presenting select summary statistics from police records, court records and prison records for residents of the East Kimberley (to the extent that this is possible for this region) this chapter will attempt some redress to this imbalance by deriving estimates of the population for whom contact with the police and a criminal conviction might represent a barrier, or at least a brake, on social and economic participation. Along the way, some sense of the nature of criminal activity and its implied impact on the social fabric will also be provided.

Data sources

Crime statistics in Western Australia are available from a variety of sources reflecting different stages of interaction with the criminal justice system. The initiating factor, of course, is contact with the police either by way of reporting a crime or via an apprehension (arrest), or summons. Such actions yield a range of data concerning the nature of offences and offenders, with separate reporting for juveniles and adults. Individuals charged with an offence are then further processed by the courts (a charge being an allegation laid by the police before the court or other prosecuting agency that a person has committed a criminal offence). Statistics relating to the activities of the lower courts (which predominate in the East Kimberley) are captured by the Department of Justice CHIPS (Children's Court and Petty Sessions) database. As for those charged who are found guilty of an offence, imprisonment data are available from the Department of Justice's Total Offender Management System (TOMS), while non-custodial community corrections data can be extracted from the records of the Community and Juvenile Justice division of the Department of Justice. Data regarding those held in police lock-ups are provided via the WA Police Lock-up Admissions System which records all admissions to and exits from police lock-ups across the state.

The Crime Research Centre (CRC) at the University of Western Australia has access to these data for analysis and reporting under agreements with the WA Police and WA Department of Justice. Using these data, the CRC produces an annual comprehensive compendium of crime and justice statistics for the State—Crime and Justice Statistics for Western Australia—detailing the nature and pattern of offences and sentences, and the characteristics of offenders and those sentenced. Among the characteristics explored is ethnicity, and the basic ethnic classification employed by the CRC in its reporting is Aboriginal/non-Aboriginal. However, the manner in which Aboriginality is determined varies between police and court data. In the Police Offence Information System (P49), 'ethnic appearance' is a term used to describe the visual appearance of victims and offenders. The field is completed on the basis of the attending police officer's subjective assessment of the person's appearance, and is recorded for operational purposes only. As the CRC cautions, given the subjective nature of the assessment upon which these data are based, it is possible that a person attributed to a particular group does not belong to that group. Data from the lower courts presents a far greater difficulty in terms of establishing Aboriginal participation in the criminal justice system: in Western Australia as a whole the Indigenous status of defendants is unknown in 85% of cases (Loh and Ferrante 2001: 20).

In addition to these problems, three other constraints on official data sources are specific to the development of a meaningful profile of offences and offenders in the study region. First of all, some data are coded to Statistical Division level, which in this case corresponds to the whole of the Kimberley region. Second, while information on outcomes from individual lower court proceedings in the East Kimberley can be obtained from the Department of Justice, the extent to which these involve usual residents of the region cannot be determined, although CRC research does suggest that the vast majority of offences are committed in the offender's region of usual residence and so, presumably, they are also tried there (Morgan and Fernandez 2002). Finally, the largest single grouping according to ethnicity in court data is that whose ethnic status is unknown, which leads to uncertainty in the actual numbers of Aboriginal as opposed to non-Aboriginal offenders. In similar fashion, prison data record only the last known address of prisoners leading to potential (and unmeasurable) error in attributing individuals to particular regions.

Reported crime

The most common crimes reported to and recorded by police in Western Australia are classified as offences against property (including burglary, property damage/arson, and motor vehicle theft), and offences against the person (including assault, sex offences, and robbery). Other less commonly reported crimes include drug offences, fraud and receiving, and good order (mostly trespass and vagrancy), while other sundry offences (mostly offences against justice procedures) make up the remainder (Fernandez and Loh (2001: 10-12). No detailed data on offences reported to police in the Northern East Kimberley exist in the public domain. However, rates of reporting for offences against the person and property offences in 2001 are available for the Kimberley as a whole. Taken together, these reveal that the Kimberley has the second highest rate of such offences (200 per thousand) of all regions in Western Australia, with the State average at 170 per thousand (Fernandez and Loh 2001: 18). These rates for the Kimberley region can be used to estimate the number of reported offences in the study region on the (untested) assumption that these rates are consistent across the Kimberley. Thus, as shown in Table 8.1, the rate of reporting assaults in the Kimberley was 26.4 per thousand. Applied to the usual resident population of the study region this translates to a total of 195 such offences. Table 8.1 also shows the estimated number of offences for all broad category offences against the person and property offences.

Table 8.1.   Estimated offences reported to and recorded by police in the Northern East Kimberley, 2001

	Kimberley rate (per thousand persons)[a]	Estimated number of offences reported in the study region[b]
Offences against the person		
Assault	26.4	195
Sex offences	3.0	22
Robbery	0.6	4
Other	3.1	23
Total against the person	33.1	244
Property offences		
Burglary		
- dwellings	24.6	182
- commercial	7.2	53
Vehicle theft	4.7	35
Other	113.9	841
Total property	150.3	1,111
Total offences	199.6	1,355

Notes: a. From Fernandez and Loh (2001: 18)
       b. Based on estimate of resident population aged 10 years and over

Reported offences in the East Kimberley

As part of an exercise in mapping crime and offenders in Western Australia for the period 1997-99, Morgan and Fernandez (2002: A29-31) derived rates of police-offender contacts for urban centres within the Kimberley and comparison of these offers some insight into the relative level of reported crime in Halls Creek, Kununurra and Wyndham urban centres vis a vis other towns in the Kimberley, and the region as a whole. One clear finding is that the Halls Creek area stands out as having by far the highest rate of Aboriginal offender contacts, with 35% of the population over 10 years apprehended. The second highest rate was reported in Kununurra with around 23%. Wyndham recorded levels around the Kimberley average of 16%. Compared to non-Aboriginal offender rates in these areas, these levels of Aboriginal police contact are astronomical—around 58 times higher in Halls Creek, 17 times higher in Kununurra, and 16 times higher in Wyndham. Also of note is the fact that offender rates for all males far exceed those of all females—by 5 times in Halls Creek, 4 times in Kununurra, and 5 times in Wyndham. As for the nature of offences reported, Halls Creek again stands out with relatively high rates of offences against the person, property offences, and good order offences—in each case far above the regional average and the levels reported in Kununurra and Wyndham. However, Kununurra recorded the highest rate of drug offences at almost 15 per thousand compared to the regional average of around 10 per thousand.

Supplementary charts to the CRC reports for the Aboriginal Justice Council also provide regional postcode data by Indigenous status (Loh and Ferrante 2001). For example, in Table 8.2, reported property offence rates are shown according to Kimberley postcode areas in 2000. The first point to note is that the rate of reported property offences is higher for non-Indigenous victims compared to Indigenous victims, although the exact extent of the difference between the two is indeterminate owing to a large number of victims whose Indigenous status is not established. The second observation is that the rate of property offences reported by Indigenous people is greatest in Kununurra and very low in Wyndham, while for non-Indigenous people reported offences are highest in Derby and Broome.

Table 8.2.   **Reported property offence rates[a] by Indigenous status of victim: Kimberley postcodes, 2000**

	Broome	Derby	Fitzroy Crossing	Halls Creek	Kununurra	Wyndham
Indigenous	60.3	25.8	17.2	27.0	61.5	10.7
Non-Indigenous	129.0	131.5	56.8	101.8	91.5	96.3
Total	162.6	145.3	75.8	168.6	131.0	103.9

Note: a. Rate per 1,000 persons

Source: Supplementary tables to Loh and Ferrante 2001

As for reported violent crime, by far the highest rates are reported by Aboriginal people in the Kununurra and Broome postcode areas (Table 8.3). In the Kununurra area, Aboriginal people report violent offences against the person at a rate 8 times higher than their non-Indigenous counterparts. This is by far the greatest discrepancy in violent crime reporting across the Kimberley. At the other extreme, Aboriginal people in the Wyndham area report relatively low rates of violent offences, and at a rate very similar to non-Aboriginal people.

Table 8.3.   Reported violent offence rates[a] by Indigenous status of victim: Kimberley postcodes, 2000

	Broome	Derby	Fitzroy Crossing	Halls Creek	Kununurra	Wyndham
Indigenous	90.5	48.5	46.6	47.1	94.7	20.1
Non-Indigenous	19.5	32.7	20.9	26.2	11.5	18.4
Total	37.9	40.6	38.2	38.3	22.1	19.4

Note: a. Rate per 1,000 persons
Source: Supplementary tables to Loh and Ferrante 2001

Contact with the police

Contact between the police and the regional population is recorded as persons are apprehended by the police (either via arrest or summons), or are diverted (as juveniles) through the cautioning system and referred to juvenile justice teams. Apprehensions data are derived from the police P18 form and describe offences charged by police either via arrest or summons. According to data reported by the CRC for 2001 (Fernandez and Loh 2001: 49), as many as 81.4% of all apprehensions recorded in the Kimberley SD involved charges laid against Aboriginal people (excluding juvenile cautions and minor traffic offences). If the number of Aboriginal apprehensions in the Northern East Kimberley is in proportion to its share of the Aboriginal population of the Kimberley as a whole (28%), then it can be estimated that a total of 1,221 such apprehensions were laid in the study region in 2001.

However, an individual may have more than one apprehension in a given year. Due to the absence of data on the number of distinct persons arrested in the Northern East Kimberley, there is a need for some creativity in applying state-level information to the regional situation. Thus, to estimate the number of distinct Aboriginal persons arrested in the study region, Aboriginal age-specific prevalence arrest rates calculated by the CRC for Western Australia as a whole can be applied to regional ERP data, although, of course, this assumes that these rates are applicable. If we start with the overall Kimberley Aboriginal prevalence arrest rate of 203.7 per thousand in 2000 (Loh and Ferrante 2001:

14), and then apply this to the Northern East Kimberley population in 2001, this produces a total of 642 Aboriginal persons arrested in the region in 2001. This figure can then be distributed according to the implied share of total arrests in each age group based on the statewide age-specific arrest rates. The result is shown in Table 8.4.

The estimated total number of juveniles arrested amounts to 90, with almost as many again in the 18-19 years age group. Most of those arrested (340, or 53%) are between 20 and 34 years of age. This number represents almost one-third (32%) of the regional population between these ages. To put this in a regional economic context, the estimated numbers arrested are far greater than the 202 persons aged between 15 and 34 who are employed in the regional mainstream labour market. Indeed, cross-reference to the relatively poor labour force status of Aboriginal people between the ages of 15 and 34 (see Chapter 3), suggests the likelihood that high arrest rates represent a major barrier to regional participation, which is not surprising given the disruption to labour market engagement that contact with the police and its subsequent consequences imply.

Table 8.4.   Estimated distinct Aboriginal persons arrested by age group: Northern East Kimberley, 2001

Age group	Regional Aboriginal population	WA Aboriginal age-specific arrest rates[a]	Implied % of arrests by age group	Estimated arrests by age group
10-14	516	54.2	5.0	32
15-17	259	195.6	9.1	58
18-19	199	320.2	11.4	73
20-24	385	296.6	20.5	132
25-29	345	292.2	18.1	116
30-34	325	245	14.3	92
35-39	273	195.3	9.5	61
40-44	202	147.8	5.4	34
45-49	178	115.8	3.7	24
50-54	120	64.5	1.4	9
55-59	107	54.7	1.1	7
60-64	78	22	0.3	2
65-69	67	13.4	0.2	1
70+	104	5.3	0.1	1
Total	3,158	–	100.0	642

Note: a. From Loh and Ferrante (2001: 13); data refer to 2000

Arrest rates in Kimberley postcode areas

Once again, the supplementary charts to the Aboriginal Justice Council reports provide a window on regional variations in arrest rates within the Kimberley (Loh and Ferrante 2001). From Table 8.5, it can be seen that arrest rates for property offences are exceedingly high among Aboriginal people in the Kununurra area. The rate of Aboriginal arrest for property offences is 60 times higher than the non-Aboriginal rate in this area. The next highest arrest rate is recorded among Aboriginal people in the Halls Creek area, and collectively arrests for property offences are far more likely to occur in the East Kimberley, rather than the West Kimberley.

Table 8.5. Arrest rates[a] for property offences by Indigenous status: Kimberley postcodes, 2000

	Broome	Derby	Fitzroy Crossing	Halls Creek	Kununurra	Wyndham
Indigenous	81.7	86.4	28.3	108.1	239.0	59.6
Non-Indigenous	7.9	8.3	4.6	5.6	4.1	4.3
Total	26.4	45.1	21.4	65.4	34.3	38.5

Note: a. Rate per 1,000 persons
Source: Supplementary tables to Loh and Ferrante 2001

A somewhat similar pattern is evident with regard to arrests for violent offences (Table 8.6) with the Kununurra area standing out as having relatively high arrest rates among Aboriginal people. In this area, the Aboriginal arrest rate for violent offences is 42 times higher than the non-Aboriginal rate. Arrest rates for good order offences refer mostly to trespass and vagrancy. Here again, the Kununurra postcode area records by far the highest rate, as does the East Kimberley region generally (Table 8.7). Aboriginal people in the Kununurra area are 45 times more likely than non-Aboriginal people to be arrested for good order offences.

Table 8.6. Arrest rates[a] for violent offences by Indigenous status: Kimberley postcodes, 2000

	Broome	Derby	Fitzroy Crossing	Halls Creek	Kununurra	Wyndham
Indigenous	52.7	44.8	37.1	44.3	101.8	17.4
Non-Indigenous	4.5	7.4	3.5	6.4	2.4	1.1
Total	16.7	25.3	26.6	28.4	15.3	11.2

Note: a. Rate per 1,000 persons
Source: Supplementary tables to Loh and Ferrante 2001

Table 8.7. **Arrest rates[a] for good order offences by Indigenous status: Kimberley postcodes, 2000**

	Broome	Derby	Fitzroy Crossing	Halls Creek	Kununurra	Wyndham
Indigenous	77.0	127.5	70.0	197.8	357.4	115.3
Non-Indigenous	9.5	12.4	1.2	28.6	7.9	9.7
Total	27.0	67.9	47.6	127.8	53.4	78.2

Note: a. Rate per 1,000 persons
Source: Supplementary tables to Loh and Ferrante 2001

In East Kimberley postcode areas, a total of 2,201 Aboriginal receivals in police lock-ups were recorded in 2000—a number equivalent to 48% of the region's Aboriginal population over 10 years of age (Table 8.8). However, it should be noted that the number of receivals exceeds the number of distinct persons, though to what extent is unknown. Of more interest is the fact that more than half (58%) of all 3,805 Aboriginal receivals into police lock-ups recorded for the Kimberley as a whole were reported in the East Kimberley, despite the fact that the East Kimberley share of the wider Kimberley population is only 39%. This spatial imbalance pointing to greater levels of police contact in the East Kimberley is consistent with the much higher arrest rates observed in this region. Together, these indicators suggest that the relative need for crime prevention resources is greater in the East Kimberley, especially in the Kununurra district.

Table 8.8. **Numbers of receivals in police lock-ups by Indigenous status: Kimberley postcodes, 2000**

	Broome	Derby	Fitzroy Crossing	Halls Creek	Kununurra	Wyndham
Indigenous	752	662	190	1,076	893	232
Non-Indigenous	345	52	3	38	117	8
Total	1,097	714	193	1,114	1,010	240

Source: Supplementary tables to Loh and Ferrante 2001

Lower Court data

Data were obtained from the Western Australian Department of Justice regarding the decision type for adjudicated cases from the Children's Courts and Courts of Petty Sessions in Kalumburu, Oombulgurri, Wyndham, Kununurra, Warmun, and Halls Creek in 2001–2002. These data were classified according to Aboriginal identification and gender. However, a major drawback for the analysis of these data is the lack of a process of ethnic self-identification with the result that out of a total of 1,584 adjudicated cases, only 22% were recorded as Aboriginal, with the ethnic identity in the vast majority of the remaining cases (77%) recorded as unknown. However, given the arrest rates described above, it can be reasonably assumed that the majority of sentences reported in these data relate to Aboriginal persons.

The distribution of adjudicated court cases by Aboriginality of offender (Petty Sessions plus Children's Courts) in the Northern East Kimberley is shown in Table 8.9. More than half of all court hearings are in Kununurra, followed by Halls Creek with almost one-third. Clearly the community-based courts in Warmun, Oombulgurri and Kalumburu play a lesser role. But this cannot be taken to indicate that residents of these places have less interaction with the court system; it is simply that their cases are more likely heard elsewhere.

Table 8.9.   Number of adjudicated cases in select East Kimberley courts[a] by Aboriginality of offender, 2001–2002

	Aboriginal		Non-Aboriginal		Unknown		Total	
	No.	%	No.	%	No.	%	No.	%
Kalumburu	18	5.3	0	0.0	75	6.1	93	5.9
Oombulgurri	3	0.9	0	0.0	2	0.2	5	0.3
Wyndham	14	4.0	0	0.0	91	7.4	105	6.6
Kununurra	207	60.5	17	89.5	612	50.0	836	52.8
Warmun	6	1.7	0	0.0	37	3.0	43	2.7
Halls Creek	94	27.5	2	10.5	406	33.2	502	31.7
Total region	342	100.0	19	100.0	1,223	100.0	1,584	100.0

Note: a. Includes Children's Courts and Courts of Petty Sessions
Source: WA Department of Justice

The findings of court proceedings in the form of penalties (sentences) can be grouped into four broad categories: custodial, non-custodial, fines and dismissals. According to the ABS sentence type classification (ABS 2003: 71), custodial orders involve custody in a correctional institution either as life imprisonment, imprisonment with a determined term, or periodic detention. They also include custody in the community under an Intensive Corrections Order or home detention. Suspended sentences also fall under custodial orders. Non-custodial orders include a variety of community supervision or work orders and community service orders, as well as probation and treatment orders. Other non-custodial orders include good behaviour bonds and recognizance orders, while monetary orders basically refer to fines or recompense to victims as well as licence disqualification/suspension/amendment and forfeiture of property.

As non-custodial sentences are the most common it is worth defining some further aspects of these. For example, Community Based Orders allow the court to order an offender to be managed by a Community Corrections Officer for the purposes of any one or more requirements of supervision, community service of between 40 to 120 hours, and/or programs aimed at the offender's behaviour. Intensive Supervision Orders are similar but provide for longer and more stringent supervision including curfews. For people who are in default of a fine, Work and Development Orders are the last option prior to imprisonment. The order requires that the offender perform a specified number of hours of community work and personal development.

In the East Kimberley, as in all remote Aboriginal communities in Western Australia, these non-custodial orders are carried out under the Aboriginal Community Supervision Agreement which offers communities a key role in the decision making about offender management. As Parriman and Daley (1999) point out, communities decide themselves whether to accept an offender under supervision, they determine who is the most appropriate person to administer the supervision order, and they are largely responsible for determining the supervision regime. One consequence has been a greater tendency on the part of the courts to make greater use of community based sentencing (Parriman and Daley 1999: 3), and this is reflected in the sentencing data for the East Kimberley.

Table 8.10 shows the distribution of penalties awarded to convicted charges in 2001–02 by the various Courts of Petty Sessions within the study region according to the type of sentence. By far the largest number of convictions (58%) attracted a monetary penalty in the form of a fine. This is followed by non-custodial sentences awarded in 32% of cases. In all, 93 cases attracted a custodial sentence, representing just 7% of all cases. However, in 2000–01, a total of 137 individuals whose last known address was in the East Kimberley were in prison, mostly in the Broome regional prison.

Table 8.10. **Distribution of penalties awarded to convicted charges by locality: Courts of Petty Sessions in the Northern East Kimberley, 2001–2002**

	Custodial		Non-custodial		Fine		Dismissal[a]	
	No.	%	No.	%	No.	%	No.	%
Kalumburu	5	5.4	17	4.1	13	1.7	7	17.1
Oombulgurri	0	0.0	3	0.7	0	0.0	0	0.0
Wyndham	13	14.0	33	8.0	44	5.8	8	19.5
Kununurra	38	40.9	227	54.8	403	53.7	3	7.3
Warmun	2	2.1	33	8.0	3	0.4	4	9.7
Halls Creek	35	37.6	101	24.4	288	38.3	19	46.3
Total region	93	100.0	414	100.0	751	100.0	41	100.0

Note: a. Includes findings of no punishment (NP46)

Source: WA Department of Justice

Not surprisingly, most cases were tried at the Kununurra court, and this is reflected in the percentage distribution of sentences handed out, although Halls Creek appears to have recorded a disproportionate share of custodial sentences based on the overall number of cases heard. A similar picture emerges from sentencing patterns in the Children's Courts (Table 8.11), with non-custodial sentences, including referrals to juvenile justice teams, accounting for 68% of all sentences. However, juvenile custodial sentences represent a higher proportion of all sentences (12%) compared to the adult courts.

Table 8.11. **Distribution of court penalties awarded to convicted charges by locality: Children's Courts in the Northern East Kimberley, 2001–2002**

	Custodial		Non-custodial		Fine		Dismissal[a]	
	No.	%	No.	%	No.	%	No.	%
Kalumburu	3	14.3	10	8.3	0	0.0	2	8.7
Oombulgurri	0	0.0	2	1.6	0	0.0	0	0.0
Wyndham	0	0.0	2	1.6	0	0.0	1	4.3
Kununurra	16	76.2	66	54.5	5	35.7	17	73.9
Warmun	0	0.0	1	0.8	0	0.0	0	0.0
Halls Creek	2	9.5	40	33.0	9	64.3	3	13.0
Total region	21	100.0	121	100.0	14	100.0	23	100.0

Note: a. Includes findings of no punishment (NP66 and NP67)

Source: WA Department of Justice

9. Implications, dilemmas, and the way ahead

The purpose of this analysis has been to portray the social and economic status of the population resident within the Northern East Kimberley at a point in time prior to either the winding down and ultimate cessation of mining activities at Argyle Diamond Mine, or the commencement of new operations and extension of the life of the mine to around 2020. To this extent, the baseline provided sits at a crossroads with options for future social and economic outcomes still the subject of negotiation between traditional owners, mine management and the State government. The value of such a profile is twofold. First, it assists by providing a quantum to discussions of need, aspirations, and regional development capacities. Second, it provides a benchmark against which the impact of any developmental decisions and future actions associated with them may be measured. Thus, the content of this report does not constitute a social impact assessment; rather it lays a foundation for identifying key requirements of regional development planning. With this in mind, the implications of the findings for each of these areas are summarised below.

Demography

It is difficult to portray the demography of the East Kimberley region as a consolidated whole. In effect there are two, even three, demographic profiles required on the basis of different population histories, composition and dynamics—one for the Aboriginal population, one for the usually resident non-Indigenous population, and one for a transitory population whose usual residence is elsewhere.

Of course, it is the Aboriginal population that has by far the longest and most enduring association with the region. From the time of their first contact with outsiders in the late nineteenth century, the Aboriginal peoples of the East Kimberley have experienced major demographic upheaval involving initial depopulation, a prolonged period of consolidation characterised by low growth, and in more recent times (since the 1970s) an expansion in numbers with high rates of growth. This recent phase of high population growth coincides with the integration of Aboriginal people into the provisions of the welfare state, and a related expansion of service provision in the region, notably in areas of health, housing and education.

As for the non-Indigenous population, usual resident numbers have also increased since the 1970s following the commencement of mining at Argyle alongside an expansion of jobs in agriculture, tourism, and related service industries, together with enhanced provision of State and local government infrastructure. This is typically a migrant population, located overwhelmingly in the region's three urban centres, and focused on working-age groups with net migration loss in the teen and older age groups.

A further by-product of the expansion of economic activity in recent years has been a growth in visitation to the region of individuals whose usual residence is elsewhere. This group includes tourists, as well as temporary workers on short-term contracts, or FI/FO arrangements. While the individuals involved might change rapidly, temporary visitors nonetheless constitute a permanent presence in the region, especially in urban centres, and particularly in the dry season.

The background to the contemporary evolution of Aboriginal settlement in the region is well documented and is not repeated here (Coombs et al. 1989: 21-50; Ross 1989; Williams and Kirkby 1989). Suffice to point out that mining activities at Argyle commenced at a time when Aboriginal people were still regrouping geographically, having been evicted from long association with pastoral properties across the region and resettling on Aboriginal reserves and pockets of Crown land in and around Kununurra, Halls Creek and Wyndham, and at Turkey Creek (later the site for Warmun community). Subsequent decades have witnessed sustained growth of the Aboriginal population and its increased dispersion throughout the region contingent on the acquisition of legally recognised tenure to traditional lands—either through the buyback of cattle stations (such as at Doon Doon and Bow River), or via reserves being handed over to Aboriginal control (such as at Turkey Creek and Violet Valley). This 'return to country' and associated development of widespread dispersed settlement has greatly extended the residential circumstances of Aboriginal people within the region. This now ranges from suburban dwellings in town alongside non-Indigenous residents and visitors, to remote camping places for small family groups.

Thus, for Aboriginal people in the region, the overriding demographic characteristic today is sustained rapid population growth and a burgeoning youthful age profile. While natural increase constitutes the primary share of this growth, some indication of net in-migration is also present. Despite social networks that create a diaspora of East Kimberley Aboriginal people across the Kimberley as a whole and into the Northern Territory, and notwithstanding frequent population mobility beyond the immediate region, for the most part individuals born within the vicinity of Argyle mine conduct their affairs and pass through life in the same area. This demographic stability reflects, in part, the strength of cultural continuity and a growing capacity to sustain chosen lifestyles. But an untested and important question is the extent to which this perceived stability also reflects an incapacity to engage wider social and economic structures, for want of adequate human capital. Such issues are likely to loom larger in the years ahead as the pressures to provide sustenance and life chances for a growing population increase.

Jobs and economic status

Against the stated aims of key Commonwealth and State policy initiatives, it is clear that economic outcomes for Aboriginal people in the Northern East Kimberley are less than optimal. Over the past 20 years, Aboriginal employment in the mainstream labour market has fallen, the Aboriginal share of total regional income has declined, and the gap between Aboriginal and non-Aboriginal residents of the region in terms of personal income levels has widened. Aboriginal people are less likely now to be participating in the workforce than before, and their levels of dependence on welfare have increased accordingly.

This conclusion has significance in light of the potential benefits and concerns expressed in regard to mine impacts in the original Ashton Joint Venture Environmental Review and Management Program (ERMP):

> The project has the potential to enhance and widen opportunities for those groups who are now regarded as disadvantaged, as well as other groups. Distributional effects of benefits will need to be considered carefully in terms of their wider social implications and not only in financial terms. (ERMP 1982: 228)

> ...if community fortunes wane, even temporarily, and stresses grow in the community as a result, there is danger that the Project will be seen as partly or wholly responsible for the change in well-being, whether it caused the changes or not. (ERMP 1982: 246)

The pity is that a measure of these costs and benefits to the regional population is only now available some 20 years on, and that they were not the subject of continuous tracking over the life of the project.

If social and economic conditions for Aboriginal people remain the same as currently experienced, then the cost to government of providing income support and other welfare payments, as well as program support in areas of health, housing and CDEP in particular, will escalate over time in line with the growth in working age population. On the other hand, if Aboriginal people had more jobs at higher occupational levels, then, from their own incomes, they would be able to meet many of the basic needs that governments now provide for. Some estimate of the opportunity cost to government of simply continuing business as usual is provided here in the form of welfare dependency rates and associated estimates of dollar amounts. What is not costed, though, is the potentially greater public impost of excess disease burden, infrastructure replacement, and foregone educational outcomes due to the continued and growing marginalisation of Aboriginal people within the regional economy. It is important to recognise that the policy options for addressing this situation are not cost neutral—expenditure will grow either in response to declining economic status, or in order to enhance it. Whatever the case, a fiscal response is unavoidable.

Alongside the consideration of options to open up areas of the regional labour market to Aboriginal employment in the same manner as is underway at Argyle mine (Argyle Diamonds 2002), there is a parallel need to tackle much deeper structural hurdles if Aboriginal people are to successfully compete for skilled mainstream jobs with other residents (and potential in-migrants, both Aboriginal and non-Aboriginal). Aside from the fact that one-quarter of the adult population was arrested in 2001, these include poor literacy and numeracy levels, which in part reflect low school participation and attendance levels—only 73% of the regional school age population is enrolled, and average retention to year 12 amounts to only 10 individuals; only 25 Aboriginal students each year achieve benchmark competencies in Year 7 reading and writing; only 132 adults have post-secondary qualifications. Also for noting is the continuing high adult morbidity and mortality—if a 15 year old Indigenous male in the region has only a 60% chance of reaching age 60, then the physical limitations on prolonged and full participation in the workforce become all too apparent, especially if we add to this the high rates of morbidity and disability that are prevalent throughout the prime working ages.

With some residual residential access to Aboriginal lands in the region, and the possibility of more in the future via native title determinations, the extent to which real lifestyle choices are being made by the local population has also to be factored into any policy response. Clearly, the existence of continuing ties to country, and the customary economic activities that stem from this, means that opportunities for economic activity should be exploited wherever they emerge. In considering such options, one issue is the extent to which the full range of existing economic activities is adequately reflected in the official census statistics presented here. For example, it would appear that many locally significant tasks are either subsumed in the census under the label of 'CDEP' or 'labouring', or overlooked altogether due to their lack of fit with mainstream labour force categories. Examples of such activity abound in the literature and are associated with aspects of customary economy (hunting, fishing and gathering), art and craft manufacture, land management and ceremonial business (Altman 2002; Altman and Whitehead 2003; Bomford and Caughley 1996), often with fledgling or well-established employment potential.

Of interest here is the fact that census records for the region identify no Aboriginal artists, actors or dancers in its official occupational classification of those employed, and yet one of the mainstream employment success stories of the region is the manner in which private sector interests have combined with traditional culture to engage numerous individuals in meaningful and gainful employment. Noteworthy examples include the Warmun Arts Centre which has an annual turnover of $1m, has 88 artists registered, and employs 18 of these full-time with earnings well above the regional average. The Warmun-based Neminuwarlum Dance group is another. It is interesting to note that such synergies, and the general importance of art and art centres in generating local employment and income, has recently been acknowledged by the Northern Territory government with their launch of a $3.2 million Indigenous Arts Strategy (Northern Territory Government 2003).

Given their labour intensive nature and widespread occurrence, it is important to consider ways of strengthening such elements of customary economic activity as part of the broad strategy of raising employment levels. To date, the primary focus for future employment growth appears to have been on mining, and not surprisingly so given ADM's targeted goals and the spread of exploration and mining activity more generally in the region such as at Sally Malay. However, set against the background of an expanding working age population, the additional work generated by such activities will be insufficient to keep up with extra demand leading to potential further deterioration of gross regional employment indicators, all other things being equal.

In the meantime, employment generation in most remote communities, and to some extent in towns as well, is most likely to occur via an import substitution model embracing activities such as the construction and maintenance of physical infrastructure, education, health services, retailing, public administration, transport, media, land restoration, land management and tourism. As argued, some of this diversity in economic activity is already in place via CDEP schemes, although it is rarely recognised as such, often being seen amorphously as 'just CDEP' work. As for community-based jobs that are currently occupied by imported non-Aboriginal workers, these tend to be managerial and professional positions with a requisite need for skills. In any case, as with mining jobs, they are insufficient in number to satisfy the growing demand for employment, even if all positions were filled by Aboriginal people.

Education and training

The polarisation of employment between Aboriginal and non-Aboriginal people that is observed in the regional labour market is mirrored, and has many of its antecedents, in terms of relative educational status. While the historic reality is that many older Aboriginal adults in the region have never attended school, it remains the case that not all of those in the current school age group are enrolled. It is estimated here that this might involve up to 25% of the regional population of compulsory school age. Among those who do enrol, their retention to year 10 is consistent with the level observed for Aboriginal students generally in Western Australia, which means that only some 15% fall away. However, retention to year 12 is a rarity and falls far below state averages. In effect, the average annual Aboriginal enrolment in year 10 in the region comprises some 60 students; in year 12 it is only ten. Not surprisingly, in 2001, the estimated number of Aboriginal adults in the region who claimed to have completed year 12 amounted to only 220, while an estimated 750 claimed year 10 level.

While the appropriate cross-tabulation has not been established, it seems reasonable to assume that these individuals would comprise a sizeable share, if not all, of the 428 Aboriginal adults estimated to be employed in the region outside of the CDEP scheme in 2001. In effect, all those with a basic competitive educational background would appear to be already in gainful mainstream employment, with as many again who are not. Any expansion of Aboriginal participation in mainstream employment would no doubt be readily taken up by the estimated 550 or so local adults who have at least year 10 level education but who were not gainfully employed in 2001. In terms of the potential for an educated Aboriginal labour supply to be sourced locally, this finding is encouraging. However, three other observations sound a note of caution.

First, it is noted that age at leaving school, and even highest year of schooling completed, does not necessarily equate with grade level achievement. To the extent that data are available to assess this, it is significant to note that only 21% of Aboriginal students in year 7 meet the benchmark in numeracy and 22% in reading, compared to figures of 81% and 85% of all students in the state. Again, in terms of actual numbers, these Aboriginal performance levels convert into an estimate of barely 25 students with benchmark competencies coming through the system each year—hardly an indication of substantial output from the local education system to feed the post-secondary training programs and future employment opportunities.

Second, somewhat similar calculations can be made in regard to VET sector output, although here the indications are more promising. While module load completion rates do not provide a direct measure of successful final outcomes in terms of producing qualified individuals, if the Aboriginal rate observed for the region is applied to Aboriginal enrolments, then this suggests a potential future output of around 300 individuals emerging from the VET system, mostly at certificate levels I to III. While this would convert to an increase in the current estimate of 130 Aboriginal adults in the region with post-secondary qualifications, many of these may well be the same people. Also, it is not known how many of those engaged in training already form part of the regional workforce, either with jobs in the mainstream or via CDEP.

Finally, the data on education and training participation and outcomes mean that local demand for Aboriginal labour as envisaged and targeted by ADM and other regional employers is likely to be matched by suitably qualified local supply. This is not least because of the efforts made by ADM itself in the area of training provision (Argyle Diamonds 2002, 2003). However, the extent of underperformance in both education and training means that the vast majority of Aboriginal adults in the region, both present and future, will be left uneducated, unqualified, unemployed, or underemployed on CDEP, and effectively marginalised in the face of any competition for jobs from more qualified countrymen or outsiders. Thus, the key regional development challenge is going to be in ensuring equitable, not just partial, participation.

Housing and infrastructure

One of the more visible manifestations of low socioeconomic status among Aboriginal residents of the north east Kimberley (and indeed across much of Australia) is the poor condition and inadequacy of housing stock and community infrastructure. This situation is exacerbated by an over-reliance on the state for the provision of housing due to the absence of a housing market in Aboriginal communities, and the inability of most Aboriginal residents in towns to service a housing loan. It is a moot point, and worth investigating, as to whether employment at Argyle leads to home purchase within the region as this would represent a significant social change. All that can be said from available data is that if this has occurred it has not been of a level to substantially alter the basic Aboriginal tenure profile which remains heavily reliant on rental accommodation.

That said, there is some confusion surrounding the distribution of Aboriginal housing tenure in the region's three towns. Data available from the Western Australia Department of Housing and Works appear substantially at odds with 2001 ABS Census data in respect of the number of State housing dwellings and other forms of public rental, with figures from the census substantially lower. As a consequence, the true distribution of urban dwellings by tenure type remains unknown, which seems remarkable for such small town settings. While this may seem a question of semantics at one level, there is a significant problem here in regard to charting the size of the housing stock available and assessing current and future need in the context of an expanding population. To take just one issue alone, if the intention of Argyle is to move away from fly-in/fly-out and shift to local sourcing of labour, what demands will this place on regional housing and what capacity is there to meet it? Such questions can only be answered with an accurate balance sheet of stocks and flows.

Leaving these uncertainties aside, it is clear that, in the 20 years since mining commenced at Argyle, the overall regional occupancy rate for Aboriginal dwellings has been reduced only slightly and remains well above the State average. This is especially so if the focus is only on community housing away from towns. Thus, it would appear that the provision of housing has only just kept ahead of increased demand due to new household formation, and has had only limited impact on the aggregate level of overcrowding. Of course averages mask diversity and there are many localities within the region, especially though not exclusively at outstations, where overcrowding levels are excessive, with up to 15 persons per dwelling. While this partly reflects larger Aboriginal families and households, and to some extent a cultural preference for extended family living arrangements, there is no doubt that the average provides a basic measure of housing inadequacy.

This is especially the case if the functionality of housing and related environmental health infrastructure is factored in. The most direct implication of poor housing and associated living conditions in the region is for health status. While direct empirical evidence linking these conditions to health outcomes is not available for this region, the positive relationship between the incidence of infectious diseases and of clean water, hygienic food preparation and storage, effective waste disposal, and reduced overcrowding is one of the more robust in the international literature and forms the basis of the epidemiological transition. In acknowledgment of this correlation, minimum standards in environmental health infrastructure are set out as part of the Commonwealth response to Indigenous housing need (Commonwealth of Australia 1999). To the extent that appropriate data are available for this region, substantial capital inputs are required just to eliminate backlogs, while extra funding will be needed to accommodate rapid population growth.

Health status

Aboriginal people in the East Kimberley region suffer the worst health status in Western Australia as measured by standard indicators of morbidity and mortality. This is true whether comparison is made with Aboriginal people in other parts of the State, or with non-Aboriginal people locally, although differentials are obviously greater when compared with the latter. Given the links that exist between employment status and ill health (Bartley 1994), it is to be expected that the poor employment outcomes observed for East Kimberley Aboriginal people are in no small measure related to their high rates of morbidity and mortality.

With reference to just one statistic—mean age at death (which currently stands at 47 years for Aboriginal people in the East Kimberley)—the physical limitations on prolonged and full participation in the workforce become all too apparent. If we add to this the fact of relatively high Aboriginal morbidity rates commencing in young adulthood and rising throughout the prime working ages, then a pattern emerges of severe physical constraints on the ability of many in the community to engage in meaningful and sustained economic activity. From a labour market perspective, it is likely that these negative effects of poor health status commence long before individuals are eligible to join the workforce as suggested by relationships, long-established, between the poor health status of Aboriginal people and below average school performance. There is also the likelihood of less direct impacts on workforce participation such as the prospect that many individuals do not seek work due to responsibilities in caring for sick relatives.

The barriers and potential solutions to improved health status for East Kimberley residents are spelt out in the Kimberley Regional Aboriginal Health Plan (Atkinson, Bridge and Gray 1999). Among the issues underlying health status, this report emphasises the significance of on-going backlogs in achieving adequate environmental health infrastructure, of the need for improved outcomes from education and training, of the difficulties of achieving better nutritional status in the population as a result of the high cost of food and low incomes, and finally the on-going debilitating effects and social disruption caused by excessive alcohol consumption. All of these issues reflect on social and economic conditions in the region that are the focus of policy intervention. Notwithstanding this, Aboriginal health outcomes in the East Kimberley remain notably behind the rest of the State and undermine the capacity for participation in regional economic development.

Crime

Research on the factors underlying high arrest rates among Aboriginal people and the effect of these on employment prospects indicates that if governments are concerned about Aboriginal social and economic wellbeing then a priority should be to ensure that they stay out of the criminal justice system (Hunter 2001; Hunter and Borland 1999). Unfortunately, in the East Kimberley, this has not occurred to date as statistics from the police and Department of Justice indicate high levels of recorded contact with police and subsequent conviction via the courts system.

While precise levels of Aboriginal recidivism are difficult to establish owing to data quality issues, the indication from the statistics available is that almost 650 Aboriginal persons in the Northern East Kimberley were arrested in 2001. Since arrest rates are higher at younger adult ages, this implies that almost one-third of the regional population between 20 and 34 years have been arrested. As for convictions, it is estimated that 75 Aboriginal people from the region would have been committed into custody by the adult lower courts in 2001, and 337 would have received a non-custodial sentence. If these orders were handed to distinct persons (an assumption only, as the actual number is unavailable) then they would be directed at 17% of the regional adult population, while the equivalent proportion for juveniles based on the same assumption would be 15%. In addition to this, an estimated total of 623 monetary fines were handed down to Aboriginal defendants from the region, though again on behalf of how many distinct persons is actually unknown.

Among the factors that contribute to high arrest rates for Aboriginal people, high unemployment (or lack of meaningful work) and poor educational achievement have been identified as the most prominent (Hunter 2001). As we have seen, both of these pre-requisites for high arrest rates are prominent in the region, indeed more so than in most other parts of Western Australia. What is especially pernicious, though, is the existence of feedback mechanisms between arrest and socio-economic conditions whereby the fact of arrest tends to reinforce disadvantage in the very factors that contribute to it. Clearly, there is a cycle here that links recidivism and reduced levels of social and economic participation, but in a fairly complex web. Admittedly, some of these threads are more implicit than explicit in the data.

For example, from the hospital separations data it is apparent that excess use of alcohol is prevalent, so it is not surprising that 62% of respondents to the NATSIS in Wunan region identified alcohol as the main local health problem (ABS 1996: 19). At the same time, high rates of injury reported in hospitalisation data are consistent with levels of assault reported to police, as is the fact that 71% of NATSIS respondents considered family violence to be a major problem (ABS 1996: 57). Such observations point to a cycle of social dysfunction at the family and community level that is reflected in the level of interaction with the criminal justice system. In turn, individual-level efforts to break into the regional labour market may be hampered by the fact that employers (such as ADM) are keen to screen out and review the employability of individuals who have a criminal record that might suggest some risk to their business and duty of care to other workers. Indeed, some perception exists (at the Warmun CDEP, for example) that just having a police record may deter some people from even looking for work. Whether this is so or not, it can certainly be stated that high levels of interaction with the criminal justice system, especially in young adult years, are less than conducive to the steady and progressive acquisition of work skills and experience that are so necessary for successful engagement with the regional economy.

Prognosis

All of the above highlights the fact that the Northern East Kimberley has a serious economic development problem: around one half of its resident adult population, representing the majority of its Aboriginal population, remains overly dependent on welfare, structurally detached from the labour market, and ill-equipped to engage it. More disconcerting, perhaps, is a prognosis that these indicators will worsen as a consequence of rapid population growth if recent trends in the rate of Aboriginal job acquisition continue, even assuming that ADM targets for local employment are met. From a policy perspective, 'business as usual' is simply insufficient to meet the expanding needs of the regional population.

Clearly, mines such as ADM can play an important part in regional development by providing a local employment base, by developing local skills, by stimulating local Indigenous business activity, by adding to the stock of regional infrastructure, and more generally by generating regional economic multipliers. However, the net impact of these inputs will be insufficient in themselves to redress the legacy of past neglect and they will not alter regional social indicators. Deficits in labour force status, income share, educational status, housing, and health among Aboriginal people in the region are of a scale that only a partnership approach to regional development involving both industry and government could hope to redress. Furthermore, the need for wider investment in regional human capital is immediate as the impost on government of sustaining the status quo in terms of welfare spending, lost tax revenue, foregone education outcomes, maintaining the criminal justice system (to say nothing of the actual costs of crime), public housing provision, and health care are high, and can only increase given the growing weight of population numbers.

References

Altman, J. 2000. 'The economic status of Indigenous Australians', *CAEPR Discussion Paper No. 193*, Centre for Aboriginal Economic Policy Research, The Australian National University, Canberra.

Altman, J.C. 2002. 'Sustainable development options on Aboriginal land: The hybrid economy in the twenty-first century', *CAEPR Discussion Paper No. 226*, Centre for Aboriginal Economic Policy Research, The Australian National University, Canberra.

Altman, J.C. and Whitehead, P.J. 2003. 'Caring for country and sustainable Indigenous development: Opportunities, constraints and innovation', paper presented at the National Landcare Conference, Darwin, 28 April–1 May 2003.

Argyle Diamonds 2002, *Community Relations Five Year Plan 2003–2007*, Argyle Diamond Mine, East Kimberley.

Argyle Diamonds 2003, *Indigenous Employment and Training Strategy 2003–2007*, Argyle Diamond Mine, East Kimberley.

Australian Bureau of Statistics (ABS) 1996. *1994 National Aboriginal and Torres Strait Islander Survey Kununurra ATSIC Region*, Cat. no. 4196.0.00.022, ABS, Canberra.

Australian Bureau of Statistics (ABS) 2000. *Housing and Infrastructure in Aboriginal and Torres Strait Islander Communities 1999, Australia*, Cat. no. 4710.0, ABS, Canberra.

Australian Bureau of Statistics (ABS) 2002a. *Population Distribution: Aboriginal and Torres Strait Islander Australians 2001*, Cat. no. 4705.0, ABS, Canberra.

Australian Bureau of Statistics (ABS) 2002b. *Deaths 2001*, Cat. no. 3302.0, ABS, Canberra.

Australian Bureau of Statistics (ABS) 2002c. *Western Australian Indigenous Profiles, 2001*, Cat. no. 2901.0, ABS, Canberra.

Australian Bureau of Statistics (ABS) 2003. *Criminal Courts*, Cat. no. 4513.0, ABS, Canberra.

Australian Bureau of Statistics (ABS) and Centre for Aboriginal Economic Policy Research (CAEPR) 1996. *1994 National Aboriginal and Torres Strait Islander Survey: Employment Outcomes for Indigenous Australians*, Cat. no. 4199.0, ABS, Canberra.

Australian Bureau of Statistics (ABS) and National Centre for Epidemiology and Population Health (NCEPH) 1997. *Occasional Paper: Self Assessed Health Status, Indigenous Australians 1994*, Cat. no. 4707.0, ABS, Canberra.

Atkinson, D., Bridge, C., and Gray, D. 1999. *Kimberley Regional Aboriginal Health Plan*, The University of Western Australia, Nedlands.

Bartley, M. 1994. 'Unemployment and ill-health: understanding the relationship', *Journal of Epidemiology and Community Health*, 48: 333–7.

Beck, E.J. 1985. *The Enigma of Aboriginal Health*, Australian Institute of Aboriginal Studies, Canberra.

Bell, M. 1992. *Demographic Projections and Forecasts in Australia: A Directory and Digest*, Australian Government Publishing Service, Canberra.

Bell, M. 2001. 'Understanding circulation in Australia', *Journal of Population Research*, 18 (1): 1–19.

Bell, M. and Maher, C. 1995. *Internal Migration in Australia 1986–1991: The Labour Force*, Australian Government Publishing Service, Canberra.

Bell, M. and Ward, G. 2000. 'Comparing temporary mobility with permanent migration', *Tourism Geographies*, 2 (1): 87–107.

BKR Walker Wayland 2001. *Feasibility Study: Wunan-East Kimberley Aboriginal Community Stores Cooperative*, BKR Walker Wayland, West Perth.

Bomford, M. and Caughey, J. (eds) 1996. *Sustainable Use of Wildlife by Aboriginal Peoples and Torres Strait Islanders*, Australian Government Publishing Service, Canberra.

Brady, M., Kunitz, S.J., and Nash, D. 1997. 'Who's definition? Australian Aborigines, conceptualisations of health and the World Health Organisation', in M. Worboys and L. Marks (eds), *Ethnicity and Health: Historical and Contemporary Perspectives*, Routledge, London.

Couzos, S., and Murray, R. 1999. *Aboriginal Primary Health Care: An Evidence-Based Approach*, Oxford University Press, Melbourne.

Colmar Brunton WA and Colmar Brunton Social Research 2002. *Kimberley Regional Justice Project Market Research*, Prepared for the WA Department of Justice, Colmar Brunton WA, West Perth.

Commonwealth of Australia 2003. *Report on Government Services 2003, Vol 1, Education Justice, Emergency Management*, Productivity Commission, Melbourne.

Coombs, H.C., McCann, H., Ross, H. and Williams, N.M. 1989. (eds) *Land of Promises: Aborigines and Development in the East Kimberley*, Aboriginal Studies Press, Canberra.

Daly, A.E. 1995. *Aboriginal and Torres Strait Islander People in the Australian Labour Market 1986 and 1991*, Cat no. 6253.0, ABS, Canberra.

Dillon, M. 1990. 'Social impact at Argyle: Genesis of a public policy', in R.A. Dixon and M.C. Dillon (eds), *Aborigines and Diamond Mining: The Politics of Resource Development in the East Kimberley Western Australia*, University of Western Australia Press, Nedlands, WA.

Dixon, R. 1990. 'In the shadow of exclusion: Aborigines and the ideology of development in Western Australia', in R.A. Dixon and M.C. Dillon (eds), *Aborigines and Diamond Mining: The Politics of Resource Development in the East Kimberley Western Australia*, University of Western Australia Press, Nedlands, WA.

Dixon, R., Elderton, C., Irvine, S., and Kirkby, I. 1990. 'A preliminary indication of some effects of the Argyle Diamond Mine on Aboriginal communities in the region', in R.A. Dixon and M.C. Dillon (eds), *Aborigines and Diamond Mining: The Politics of Resource Development in the East Kimberley Western Australia*, University of Western Australia Press, Nedlands, WA.

Divarakan-Brown, C. 1985. 'Premature ageing in the Aboriginal community', *Proceedings of the Annual Conference of the Australian Association of Gerontology*, 20: 33-4.

Fernandez, J.A., and Loh, N.S.N. 2001. *Crime and Justice Statistics for Western Australia: 2001*, Crime Research Centre, The University of Western Australia, Crawley, WA.

Government of Western Australia 1998. *Environmental Health Needs of Aboriginal Communities in Western Australia: The 1997 Survey and its Findings*, Department of Aboriginal Affairs, Perth.

Government of Western Australia 2003. *Indicators of Regional Development in Western Australia*, Department of Local Government and Regional Development, Perth.

Gracey, M. and Spargo, R.M. 1987. 'The state of health of Aborigines in the Kimberley region', *Medical Journal of Australia*, 146: 200–4.

Gracey, M. and Spargo, R.M. 1989. 'Community-based illness in Kimberley Aborigines', *East Kimberley Working Paper No. 26*, Centre for Resource and Environmental Studies, The Australian National University, Canberra.

Harvey, B. 2002. 'New competencies in mining: Rio Tinto's experience', Paper presented at the Council of Mining and Metallurgical Congress, Cairns, 27–28 May 2002.

Holman, C.D.J., Armstrong, B.K., Arias, L.N., et al. 1990. *The Quantification of Drug-Caused Mortality and Morbidity in Australia, 1988*, Department of Community Services and Health, Canberra.

Hunter, B.H. 1996. 'The determinants of Indigenous employment outcomes: The importance of education and training', *CAEPR Discussion Paper No. 115*, Centre for Aboriginal Economic Policy Research, The Australian National University, Canberra.

Hunter, B.H. 2001. *Factors Underlying Indigenous Arrest Rates*, NSW Bureau of Crime Statistics and Research, Attorney General's Department, Sydney.

Hunter, B., and Borland, J. 1999. 'The effect of arrest on Indigenous employment prospects', *Crime and Justice Bulletin*, No. 45, NSW Bureau of Crime Statistics and Research, Attorney General's Department, Sydney.

Hunter, B.H. and Daly, A.E. 1998. 'Labour market incentives among Indigenous Australians: The cost of job loss versus the gains from employment', *CAEPR Discussion Paper No. 159*, Centre for Aboriginal Economic Policy Research, The Australian National University, Canberra.

Hunter, B.H. and Schwab, R.G. 2003. 'Practical reconciliation and recent trends in Indigenous education', *CAEPR Discussion Paper No. 249*, Centre for Aboriginal Economic Policy Research, The Australian National University, Canberra.

Jones, R. 1994. *The Housing Need of Indigenous Australians, 1991*, Research Monograph No. 8, Centre for Aboriginal Economic Policy Research, The Australian National University, Canberra.

Kakadu Region Social Impact Study 1997. *Report of the Aboriginal Project Committee*, Office of the Supervising Scientist, Canberra.

Kimberley Development Commission 1997. *Kimberley Region Western Australia Economic Development Strategy 1997–2010*, Kimberley Development Commission, Kununurra.

Kesteven, S. 1986. 'The project to monitor the social impact of uranium mining on Aboriginal communities in the Northern Territory' *Australian Aboriginal Studies*, 1986 (1): 43–5.

Kinfu, Y. and Taylor, J. 2002. 'Estimating the components of Indigenous population change, 1996-2001, *CAEPR Discussion Paper No. 243*, Centre for Aboriginal Economic Policy Research, The Australian National University, Canberra.

Lester, I.A. 1994. *Australia's Food and Nutrition*, Australian Government Publishing Service, Canberra.

Loh, N. and Ferrante, A. 2001. *Aboriginal Involvement in the Western Australia Criminal Justice System: A Statistical Review, 2000*, Report for the Aboriginal Justice Council, Crime Research Centre, The University Of Western Australia, Crawley, WA.

Martin, D. and Taylor, J. 1996. 'Ethnographic perspectives on the enumeration of Aboriginal people in remote Australia', *Journal of the Australian Population Association*, 13 (1): 17–33.

Memmott, P. and Meltzer, A. 2003. 'Social capital in Aboriginal Australia: A case study in Wadeye, Northern Territory', Paper presented at the Australian Anthropological Society Annual Conference, 1–3 October, 2003, Camperdown campus, University of Sydney.

Morgan, F. and Fernandez, J. 2002. *Mapping Crime, Offenders and Socio-Demographic Factors: Statistical Update, 1997–1999*, Crime Research Centre, The University of Western Australia, Crawley, WA.

Morphy, F. 2002. 'When systems collide: The 2001 Census at a Northern Territory outstation', in D. Martin, F. Morphy, W. Sanders and J. Taylor, *Making Sense of the Census: Observations of the 2001 Enumeration in Remote Aboriginal Australia*, Research Monograph No. 22, Centre for Aboriginal Economic Policy Research, The Australian National University, Canberra.

Nassar, N. and Sullivan E.A. 2002. *Australia's Mothers and Babies*, Australian Institute of Health and Welfare, Canberra.

Northern Territory Government 2003. *Building Strong Arts Business: Northern Territory Indigenous Arts Strategy*, Northern Territory Department of Community Development, Sport and Cultural Affairs, Darwin.

Palmer, K. and Williams, N.M. 1980. 'Aboriginal Relationships to Land in the Southern Blatchford Escarpment Area of the East Kimberley', Results of a preliminary anthropological investigation conducted under the direction of the Australian Institute of Aboriginal Studies on behalf of the Warmun Community, The Mandangala Outstation, and the Western Australian Museum, Australian Institute of Aboriginal Studies, Canberra.

Parriman, F. and Daley, D. 1999. 'Aboriginal Community Supervision Agreements in Western Australia', Paper presented at the *Best Practice Interventions in Corrections for Indigenous People Conference*, convened by the Australian Institute of Criminology and the Department of Correctional Services SA, 13-15 October 1999, Adelaide.

Pholeros, P., Rainow, S. and Torzillo, P. 1993. *Housing for Health: Towards a Healthy Living Environment for Aboriginal Australia*, Health Habitat, Newport Beach.

Ross, H. 1989. 'Community social impact assessment: A cumulative study in the Turkey Creek area, Western Australia', *East Kimberley Working Paper No. 27*, Centre for Resource and Environmental Studies, The Australian National University, Canberra.

Ross, H. 1990. 'Progress and prospects in Aboriginal social impact assessment', *Australian Aboriginal Studies*, 1990 (1): 11–17.

Rowse, T. 1988. 'From houses to households? The Aboriginal Development Commission and economic adaptation by Alice Springs town campers', *Social Analysis*, 24 (4): 50–66.

Sanders, W. 2002. 'Adapting to circumstance: The 2001 census in the Alice Springs town camps', in D. Martin, F. Morphy, W. Sanders and J. Taylor, *Making Sense of the Census: Observations of the 2001 Enumeration in Remote Indigenous Australia*, Research Monograph No. 22, Centre for Aboriginal Economic Policy Research, The Australian National University, Canberra.

Schwab, R.G. 1995. 'The calculus of reciprocity: Principles and implications of Aboriginal sharing', *CAEPR Discussion Paper No. 100*, Centre for Aboriginal Economic Policy Research, The Australian National University, Canberra.

Schwab, R.G. 1998. 'Educational "failure" and educational "success" in an Aboriginal community', *CAEPR Discussion Paper No. 161*, Centre for Aboriginal Economic Policy Research, The Australian National University, Canberra.

Senior, K.A. 2003. A Gudbala Laif? Health and Well-Being in a Remote Aboriginal Community, PhD thesis, The Australian National University, Canberra.

Sidoti, C. 2000. 'Education – the litmus of rural well-being', Address to the First National Conference on *A Future for Rural Towns*, The Regional Institute, 28 June 2000, Bendigo.

Smith, D.E. 1991. 'Toward an Aboriginal household expenditure survey: Conceptual, methodological and cultural considerations', *CAEPR Discussion Paper No. 10*, Centre for Aboriginal Economic Policy Research, The Australian National University, Canberra.

Taylor, J. 1998. 'Measuring short-term population mobility among Indigenous Australians: Options and implications', *Australian Geographer*, 29 (1): 125–37.

Taylor, J. 2001. 'Implementing Regional Agreements: Issues for regional planning', Paper presented at the Rio Tinto Aboriginal and Community Relations Conference, April 2001, Argyle Diamond Mine, East Kimberley.

Taylor, J. and Bell, M. 2001. 'Towards a composite estimate of Cape York's Indigenous population', *QCPR Discussion Paper No. 1*, Queensland Centre for Population Research, University of Queensland, St Lucia, Qld.

Taylor, J. and Bell, M. 2003. 'Options for benchmarking ABS population estimates for Indigenous communities in Queensland', *CAEPR Discussion Paper No. 243*, Centre for Aboriginal Economic Policy Research, The Australian National University, Canberra.

Taylor, J. Bern, J. and Senior, K. 2000. *Ngukurr at the Millennium: A Baseline Profile for Social Impact Planning in South-East Arnhem Land*, Research Monograph No. 18, Centre for Aboriginal Economic Policy Research, The Australian National University, Canberra.

Taylor, J. and Hunter, B. 1998. *The Job Still Ahead: Economic Costs of Continuing Indigenous Employment Disparity*, ATSIC, Canberra.

Taylor, J. and Westbury, N. 2000. *Aboriginal Nutrition and the Nyirranggulung Health Strategy in Jawoyn Country*, Research Monograph No. 19, Centre for Aboriginal Economic Policy Research, The Australian National University, Canberra.

Unwin, E., Codde, J., Swensen, G., and Saunders, P. 1997. *Alcohol-Caused Deaths and Hospitalisation in Western Australia by Health Services*, Health Department Western Australia and WA Drug Abuse Strategy Office, Perth.

Watson, J, Ejueyitsi, V.B., and Codde, J.P. 2001. 'A comparative overview of Aboriginal health in Western Australia', *Epidemiology Occasional Paper 15*, Department of Health, Perth.

Western Australia Ministry of Planning 2000. *Western Australia Tomorrow: Population Projections for the Statistical Divisions, Planning Regions and Local Government Areas of Western Australia*, Ministry of Planning Population Report No. 4, Perth.

Williams, N.M., and Kirkby, I. 1989. 'Summary of findings and recommendations. Ethnography of the East Kimberley: Location and status of Aboriginal communities', *East Kimberley Working Paper No. 33*, Centre for Resource and Environmental Studies, The Australian National University, Canberra.

Willis, J. 1995. 'Fatal attraction: Do high technology treatments for end stage renal disease benefit Aboriginal people in Central Australia?' *Australian and New Zealand Journal of Public Health*, 19 (6): 603–9.

CAEPR Research Monograph Series

1. *Aborigines in the Economy: A Select Annotated Bibliography of Policy-Relevant Research 1985–90*, L.M. Allen, J.C. Altman, and E. Owen (with assistance from W.S. Arthur), 1991.

2. *Aboriginal Employment Equity by the Year 2000*, J.C. Altman (ed.), published for the Academy of Social Sciences in Australia, 1991.

3. *A National Survey of Indigenous Australians: Options and Implications*, J.C. Altman (ed.), 1992.

4. *Indigenous Australians in the Economy: Abstracts of Research, 1991–92*, L.M. Roach and K.A. Probst, 1993.

5. *The Relative Economic Status of Indigenous Australians, 1986–91*, J. Taylor, 1993.

6. *Regional Change in the Economic Status of Indigenous Australians, 1986–91*, J. Taylor, 1993.

7. *Mabo and Native Title: Origins and Institutional Implications*, W. Sanders (ed.), 1994.

8. *The Housing Need of Indigenous Australians, 1991*, R. Jones, 1994.

9. *Indigenous Australians in the Economy: Abstracts of Research, 1993–94*, L.M. Roach and H.J. Bek, 1995.

10. *The Native Title Era: Emerging Issues for Research, Policy, and Practice*, J. Finlayson and D.E. Smith (eds), 1995.

11. *The 1994 National Aboriginal and Torres Strait Islander Survey: Findings and Future Prospects*, J.C. Altman and J. Taylor (eds), 1996.

12. *Fighting Over Country: Anthropological Perspectives*, D.E. Smith and J. Finlayson (eds), 1997.

13. *Connections in Native Title: Genealogies, Kinship, and Groups*, J.D. Finlayson, B. Rigsby, and H.J. Bek (eds), 1999.

14. *Land Rights at Risk? Evaluations of the Reeves Report*, J.C. Altman, F. Morphy, and T. Rowse (eds), 1999.

15. *Unemployment Payments, the Activity Test, and Indigenous Australians: Understanding Breach Rates*, W. Sanders, 1999.

16. *Why Only One in Three? The Complex Reasons for Low Indigenous School Retention*, R.G. Schwab, 1999.

17. *Indigenous Families and the Welfare System: Two Community Case Studies*, D.E. Smith (ed.), 2000.

18. *Ngukurr at the Millennium: A Baseline Profile for Social Impact Planning in South-East Arnhem Land*, J. Taylor, J. Bern, and K.A. Senior, 2000.

19. *Aboriginal Nutrition and the Nyirranggulung Health Strategy in Jawoyn Country*, J. Taylor and N. Westbury, 2000.

20. *The Indigenous Welfare Economy and the CDEP Scheme*, F. Morphy and W. Sanders (eds), 2001.

21. *Health Expenditure, Income and Health Status among Indigenous and Other Australians*, M.C. Gray, B.H. Hunter, and J. Taylor, 2002.

22. *Making Sense of the Census:Observations of the 2001 Enumeration in Remote Aboriginal Australia*, D.F. Martin, F. Morphy, W.G. Sanders and J. Taylor, 2002.

For information on CAEPR Discussion Papers, Working Papers and Research Monographs please contact:

Publication Sales, Centre for Aboriginal Economic Policy Research,
The Australian National University, Canberra, ACT, 0200

Telephone: 02–6125 8211
Facsimile: 02–6125 2789

Information on CAEPR abstracts and summaries of all CAEPR print publications and those published electronically can be found at the following WWW address:

http://www.anu.edu.au/caepr/